ADVANCE PRAISE FOR
SITTING PRETTY

"Rebekah Taussig's writing is a gift that keeps giving. Her voice is honest, vulnerable, and welcoming. Rebekah writes about the future she would like to see and share with all of us—and the work it will take to create it together. Much of that work is in listening to others and their lived experiences, and it was a joy to read and listen to Rebekah's words. This beautiful book helped me ask questions, open my heart, and remind me to look more closely at the world around me and what small part we can all have in making it a better, more accessible one."

—Grace Bonney, founder of Design*Sponge and
author of *In the Company of Women*

"*Sitting Pretty* is the book I needed years ago as I grappled with my sense of self and my identity as a disabled woman. I put it down while reading only long enough to collect myself each time waves of emotion crashed over me. Rebekah's spunky, self-aware wit, combined with education that never feels didactic, makes this book a worthwhile and rewarding read."

—Emily Ladau, writer, speaker, and disability rights activist

"A compelling personal book whose confidential voice leads the reader into the author's vividly lived world of disability. Smart and funny, *Sitting Pretty* does double duty, revealing not only the intimate life of a disabled woman but the flaws of the world around her that seeks to repress and contain her."

—Lennard J. Davis, Distinguished Professor at
the University of Illinois at Chicago and author of
Enforcing Normalcy and *My Sense of Silence:
Memoirs of a Childhood with Deafness*

"Rebekah writes in a way that is somehow both world-shakingly profound and beautifully intimate. Her voice is unforgettable in its power to make you feel, question, learn, and grow. There aren't words for how much the world needs this book."

—Megan Jayne Crabbe, bestselling author of
Body Positive Power

"Taussig goes beyond empty inspirational jargon, forcing readers to consider the value of the real-world improvements that can emerge from centering underrepresented voices. An engaging, up-close view of the need for structural change regarding disabilities in this country, *Sitting Pretty* is a solid combination of theory and personal experience."

—*Kirkus Reviews* (starred review)

SITTING PRETTY

SITTING PRETTY

THE VIEW FROM MY ORDINARY
RESILIENT DISABLED BODY

Rebekah Taussig

HarperOne
An Imprint of HarperCollinsPublishers

HarperCollins books may be purchased for educational, business,
or sales promotional use. For information, please email the Special Markets Department at SPsales@harpercollins.com.

FIRST EDITION

Designed by Janet Evans-Scanlon

Library of Congress Cataloging-in-Publication Data

Names: Taussig, Rebekah, author.
Title: Sitting pretty : the view from my ordinary resilient disabled
    body / Rebekah Taussig.
Description: First edition. | New York, NY : HarperOne, 2020
Identifiers: LCCN 2019056133 | ISBN 9780062936790 (hard-
    cover) | ISBN 9780062936813 (ebook)
Subjects: LCSH: Taussig, Rebekah. | Paraplegics—United
    States—Biography. | Women with disabilities—United
    States—Biography. | Disabilities.
Classification: LCC RC406.P3 T38 2020 | DDC 362.4/3092
    [B]—dc23
LC record available at https://lccn.loc.gov/2019056133

20 21 22 23 24   LSC   10 9 8 7 6 5 4 3 2 1

To everyone with a body that has been sent to the margins.
Our stories matter.

CONTENTS

PREFACE

Before we talk about anything else, can we just start with awe?
I am completely in awe of this moment we're having right
now—you and me. When I was younger, disability didn't seem
to exist outside my visits to the hospital and seating clinics
for repairs on my wheelchair. For the most part, I felt really
really weird, and not in a cool, MTV's Daria sort of way. I'd
never considered disability an identity worth understanding,
let alone celebrating, and I was pretty sure I was the only one
who experienced the world from this seat on the margins. But
here we are with this little book between us, and my mind is
blown, because either (1) you, too, were on the outside and
you're here for stories that give language to that experience,
or (2) you weren't on the outside, but you want to understand
what that feels like, and really, either way, the fact that you're
here at all changes everything. Because this right here, you and
me, looking at these stories together? This is one of the most
beautiful parts of being a human—the drive to connect and
understand, heal and blossom. This is the kernel that takes my
breath away. The piece I want to hold on to.

But first! You should know what you're getting into. Who is this person whose voice you're choosing to listen to for the next however many precious minutes of your life? And why did she write these pages? Very good questions.

You might know me from my Instagram account @sitting_ pretty. Although social media seems to find ways to destroy us on the daily, it does offer us at least one tremendous gift: the power to share a story without going through the gatekeepers who've historically said, "Pass! We don't tell those kinds of stories. Who would listen?" Almost five years ago, I started an Instagram account where I could share mini-memoirs narrating life in a body that's rarely represented, let alone represented with nuance. I'd been writing essays, sending them out whenever I could bear the vulnerability of it, and hoping some editor would happen to care about this perspective, when my roommate Bertie told me to take them to the Interwebs. Would anyone care? Maybe not. But I didn't have anything to lose. I brainstormed cheesy handles on an actual napkin that came with my cup of coffee. I played with words like "wheelchair" and "cripple" and "disabled" until I landed on the feminine, the playful, the subtly subversive @sitting_pretty—a name to highlight that I am moving around down here and doing just fine.

I started sharing little bits and scraps from my days—the layers of anxiety I carry when I shop at a grocery store, the flash of shame and warmth of intimacy born through the vulnerability of struggling to walk in front of a chosen few, the frustration and reverence I feel at the sight of my scrawny, scabby legs in the morning or soaking in the bathtub—so many stories that felt entirely singular, deeply personal, and painfully, wholeheartedly honest. I'm pretty sure my eyes popped out on springs like a cartoon when I realized there were people who wanted to listen. Some said, "Me, too!" Others said, "I had no idea!" Either way, they were invested, and I was amazed.

It was in this space that I found so many people with stories I hungered for. I didn't even realize how starved I was until I sat at the feet and listened to the stories of other disabled folks, collecting words I'd never heard, words I didn't know I could have. Their accounts deepened my understanding of my own history and gave me new pictures to reimagine what it can mean to be a disabled woman. I pictured my younger self, making up dances in my dress-up clothes. What would have happened if these stories had played a part in shaping my early perceptions? What else might I have dreamed for myself? I voiced this angsty sentiment to one of my first and favorite disabled friends in this Instagram space, Erin Clark (@erinunleashes), and she was quick to remind me that our lives aren't over. We are here now—for story-expanding, collaborative meaning-making, and starting a #CripplePunk girl band of thirty-somethings.

So here I am, writing this book, because my life isn't over, because the stories of disabled folks are so often distorted to fit someone else's louder story, because I wish I'd had any stories when I was growing up—like any at all—that represented my actual, lived experiences, because there's another generation of exquisite people growing up disabled or about to become disabled, and stories are fucking *powerful*.

A few housekeeping details to sort out before we go any farther together:

- This book is not a how-to guide, as in *How to Interact with Your Disabled Neighbor.* Sorry! Not my thing.

- I am not—by any stretch of the imagination—the representative of all disabled people. That's not a thing. The fact that I have a very visible disability (turns out it's difficult to overlook a wheelchair), and the fact that I was disabled at a very young age, changes the way you and I experience this body of mine. Even folks who share these same traits will have their own slant on what it means to them, because the experience of disability is as varied as the experiences of childbirth or breakups—there are at least seven billion different ways this could go, and even within one person, feelings can contradict or change over time. Disability expands into every possible corner and intersects with every other identity. I would be doing all of us a great disservice if I led you to believe that the conversation starts and ends with bodies and experiences that look just like mine.

- This book isn't exhaustive. In fact, I hope it sparks more conversations and more listening to more voices. I am much more comfortable in the position

of storyteller and question-asker than rule-enforcer
or final-word-sayer.

So. Here we are—you and me and all my sloppy awe. I'm terrified, eager, and a little nauseous to invite you so fully into my
world, but I think it's worth the risk. So let's go forth. Let's peel
back the layers, look with an unwavering gaze, ask the impossible questions, break our hearts, laugh at it all, and open ourselves
up for new growth. I think we're ready.

SITTING PRETTY

1

WHAT'S THE PROBLEM?

A few months ago at a big family gathering, my older brother David asked me about my writing. As we squeezed around the long table of food taking up most of my parents' living room, scooping mashed potatoes and corn casserole onto our plates, he turned to me and said, "What is your writing about? What do you hope it will bring to the world?" He's a question-asker, my brother. It can feel a bit like a job interview—think on your feet, quick! There's no time for deliberation; the next question is already on its way! But he also offered this invitation to be seen that I both crave and shrink from, because I feel deeply connected to and also wildly different from my family. I wanted to hold up the honest truth of myself for him to witness. I also tensed my muscles in preparation of being benevolently misunderstood.

I'm the youngest of six kids, each of us born about two years after the other. (That's right! With the exception of your girl here, my family produces an abundance of offspring.) Right before I was born, my parents moved from their low-income apartment complex—a three-bedroom unit filled with themselves, their five children, and several rabbits—to a tall, early twentieth-century house painted a color my mom likes to call "baby-diarrhea yellow." Back in the day, the Taussigs existed on a plane all their own. They never locked their front door, and neighborhood kids traipsed in and out like it was an extension of their own homes. They didn't believe in wearing seat belts or washing their hands before dinner. After all, if God wanted you to die in a car accident, no piddly seat belt would make any difference, and exposure to germs made you hardier. They ran around delivering homemade baskets of flowers and candy to all their neighbors on May Day, held their (unwashed) hands in prayer before dinner, and played outside without shoes. The cancer I was diagnosed with at fourteen months old; the violent chemotherapy, radiation, and surgical treatments; and my eventual paralysis at age three didn't change any of this. For good or for bad, growing up in the Taussig family meant no wallowing, no time for grieving, and definitely no whining.

When I became paralyzed, the baby-diarrhea yellow house didn't undergo any accommodations. My parents didn't install ramps or handrails, and it was several years before I got my first wheelchair. I continued to sleep on the top bunk of the top floor of the house. I learned how to pull my body up the side of my bunk bed, my feet mere props as I used my arms to lift myself up higher and higher until I tumbled onto the top mattress. I crawled on hands and knees across the patchy grass and cracked cement sidewalks to my neighbor's house, and when she wasn't home, I sat in the mud and made little bowls and cups with the clay. I started learning how to use a catheter to empty my bladder before I learned subtraction.

My three brothers and two sisters lived this with me, sleeping in the bunk bed below or beside, squeezing my hands and squinting through the nightly prayer at the dinner table, all eight of us piling into the 1976 five-passenger Ford LTD we called Hazel, making muddy magic potions together in the backyard. We lived our days climbing over each other like puppies in a box—side by side, wrestling to the ground, elbows smooshed against rib cages. It didn't occur to us to talk about my differences. (Unless it was to play pranks on strangers in Walmart by leaving me and my wheelchair overturned on the ground, wailing and waiting for people to rush to my aid, which we definitely did. Although, in retrospect, I don't know why we thought this was so hilarious.) Only much later did I realize how little we knew about ourselves, let alone each other. As close as bubbles in a glass of soda and as far away as Pluto from Earth.

During this window of crawling in the mud and scrambling up to my top bunk, I believed that I was royally beautiful, valuable, and fully capable of contributing to the group. Isn't that interesting?—to feel the most regal during the days of mud and clambering and scooting across the floor? I choreographed my own weird, passionate dances, wore frilly dress-up gowns around town, and pretended I was married to the prince. I felt talented and dreamed big. I floated in my own bubble, a universe where everything glistened and glowed and I wore a crown sparkling with jewels. I believed everything I did—the way I moved my body, the way I looked, the roundabout paths I took—was right. I'd figured out how to do all the things I wanted, and I didn't see my methods as strange or sad.

I knew that kids I didn't know stared at me, that adults directed giant, sympathetic smiles toward me, that I prompted tears and applause, but I hadn't yet pieced together that I didn't fit. The fact that I couldn't walk like the kids in my class, that I wore a clunky mess of plastic, metal, and Velcro braces on my legs, used a battered aluminum walker, and sped around on my hot-pink wheelchair, didn't really seem worth factoring into my evaluation of myself.

At least, not at first. It didn't take long at all before I began to believe different things about myself. After only a few years out in the world—going to school, playing at the park and the pool, tagging along with my dad on his Saturday-morning grocery runs—a narrative started to take shape before me—a hazy image that sharpened with time. First, I started to see myself as a burden on the people around me. Unlike all the other kids, being with me required alternate routes and problem-solving. I saw it everywhere. Hanging out with me meant having limited options on the playground, collaborating with Dad muscles to get me into a friend's house, enduring very long bathroom breaks, and helping me carry my lunch tray. I calculated that people spending time with me cost them something extra, and I wanted to spare them that high price. Starting around the age of eight, I cut friends out of my life as soon as I sensed my presence caused any extra strain.

Soon I started to believe I was ugly. My body looked so different from the bodies we'd all been taught to admire (including my long, Taussig nose—I mean, I could've designed a time machine with all of the hours I agonized over that thing). There weren't any paralyzed girls or women included in the stories told on screens, through ads, or in magazine pages. I consumed and digested the culture around me and slowly learned, with certainty, that I was not among those who would be needed, admired, wanted, loved, dated, or married. Not too much later, I began to see myself as weak and helpless, too. With the exception of Walmart greeters who, according to my child brain, didn't seem to *do* anything, I didn't see or know disabled people who were employed. I couldn't picture supporting myself with a "real" job or being able to pay my own bills.

Most of what I saw of life felt powerfully, intrinsically inaccessible to me—how was I supposed to enter those spaces, let alone contribute in them? My glistening, glowing bubble had deflated into a spot of suds evaporating on the sidewalk. This was not my universe at all. Not only did I discover I wasn't the princess, but I was an uninvited intruder, a problem to push out of sight.

This overwhelming history towered behind me as I tried to answer David's question still hovering between us: "What is your writing about? What do you hope it will bring to the world?" My brain froze as my mouth started babbling, trying to synthesize, condense, smooth out the edges of some kind of response I could hand him. *Well, I write about disability and lack of representation and the impact of inaccessibility and stigma and unemployment and … and … and.* I was like a woman trying to make spaghetti in the dark, destroying the kitchen as I grabbed every ingredient in the cupboard just in case it happened to be the one I needed. In the midst of my verbal wandering, I inevitably reached for the word "shame"—the box where I had lived for so very long, the box I still find myself tumbling back into with less provocation than I'd like to admit. This is the shame that attaches so easily to a body that doesn't fit, the shame that buds, blossoms, and consumes when you believe that your existence is a burden, a blemish on the well-oiled machine of Society.

I tried to explain to David how much I want my writing to meet people in that shame, to lift the veil and point to the source, to remind folks that their disabled bodies are not The Problem here, to hold up a flag that says, "You are not alone!" He interjected. "Shame?? You felt ashamed? How? When? Why would you ever feel that way?" He seemed troubled and confused by this word, which caught me off guard. I have done so much work to understand my intimate relationship with shame. And my own brother, who grew up beside me—one bunk bed over, one seat behind, just across the table—didn't even know. He seemed wholly unaware that as we grew up, I had come to see my body as a glaring problem, a weight on the world, a failed prototype. How could he not know?

When I really think about it, I expect most people watching my life would be surprised to learn about my long-standing relationship with shame. No one ever bullied or abused me or made fun of me to my face. This was not the case for a lot of kids growing up at the same time—is still not the case for so many kids, disabled or not, who are marginalized for any number of reasons. I know I was spared a lot, in large part because I was a cute, thin, articulate, middle-class white girl. It was also a time when everyone was taught that you're *supposed* to be nice to the disabled kid. Only the worst bullies on the after-school specials or Hallmark Channel would dare to be so vile as to make fun of the "handicapped" kid. The nondisabled protagonist would get very outraged if this ever happened. He would give a fiery speech and rebuke the villain who'd stepped so grotesquely over the line. I never once heard a person describe me as a "burden" or "ugly" or "weak" or even "lame." (Well, maybe once. But *once*? Is that really enough to hijack a person's entire sense of self?) In fact, people often used positive words to describe me, like "joyful" and "bright" and "inspirational." By all accounts, I should have had a hearty sense of self-worth. My brother David was confident that I did. So where do we point out blame when our favorite villains, Overt Cruelty and Malicious Intent, are found to be missing in action? How do we begin to understand what happened?

One short answer is *ableism*.

I didn't use this word when talking with David. Later, I wondered why. It's efficient and holds so much. It's the perfect word to answer the question at hand. What's the hesitation? I suppose that I feel a bit of caution whenever using this word with anyone who isn't already intimately familiar with its texture. Without knowing what it feels like to live inside it—the slippery surface, the sharp cuts and dull bruises it leaves—"ableism" can feel like just another "ism" in a long list that people are already weary of tracking. As a high school teacher, I watch my students' eyes glaze over or drift to the window whenever the topic comes up. The word seems to shut off curiosity—it sounds familiar enough that we're confident we already, pretty much, understand it.

It feels like a risk relying on the word "ableism," but I want to use it here, because I'm hoping to assemble something with you—something big and intricate—and in order to do that, we need some building blocks—language big enough to hold stories, allow for intellectual exploration, and keep track of patterns.

My definition of ableism is a little different from the one in the *Oxford English Dictionary*, which simply says, "Discrimination in favour of able-bodied people." Based on my decades of experience and a whole lot of reading of disability studies scholars, I find this definition insufficient. First, it's built on the assumption that there *is* a distinct category of "able-bodied" people. While language that makes distinct categories can be useful (you'll sometimes see me use the term "nondisabled" to illustrate larger patterns), relying too heavily on this black-and-white definition of "able-bodied" is dangerously misleading. It breezes much too easily over the inherent ambiguity built into having a body. "Able-bodied" invites images of ruddy-cheeked farm boys lifting bricks up ladders. Who are these people? And really, how many of us fit sturdily in this category? The legal definition of disability written into the 1990 Americans with Disabilities Act highlights the fact that disability is a far-reaching word that can attach itself to all sorts of bodies, many of them that appear perfectly "able" or are exceptionally able in one area but not as much in another. In fact, our ruddy-cheeked farm boy might also have seizures a few times a year or bipolar disorder or be somewhere on the autism spectrum. The images that come to mind when we use a word like "able-bodied" are just too one-dimensional to be terribly useful.

The *Oxford English Dictionary* definition also leaves little room for one vital piece of the story: disability is shaped just as much, if not more, by context than by the body. For example, before spectacles were invented, our population included a much greater number of people categorized as blind. Technology has changed the experience of so many bodies, and as eyeglasses have become integrated into our fashion industry, the stigma around vision that deviates from the "ideal" 20/20 has shifted. (In fact, I've owned a decent number of fake eyeglasses in my day. It's a real thing.) We don't tend to equate a person wearing glasses with "disability," even if that same person would have been considered disabled in another time and place.

And finally, people are often shifting in and out of a "disabled" state; they break a limb or get the flu or have horrible period cramps or become pregnant or (gasp!) age, and suddenly they find themselves experiencing disabling limitations. If we live long enough, all of us, without exception, will become disabled. This is a prerequisite to having, living in, being a body. The idea that some of us are firmly fixed in the "able-bodied" category is a fiction. A world built on speed, productivity, more, more, more! and far too few bathrooms (and bathroom breaks) does not consider or care for the actual bodies we live in. In other words, ableism affects all of us, whether we consider ourselves disabled or not. Because the disabled body is most powerfully affected by ableism, it is the first to cast a light on the structure, to resist and protest it, to call for its public execution, but we're all living under its dictates. Ableism punishes all of us.

In its most boiled-down, squished together, simplified form, *ableism is the process of favoring, fetishizing, and building the world around a mostly imagined, idealized body while discriminating against those bodies perceived to move, see, hear, process, operate, look, or need differently from that vision.* Often, the greater the deviation, the greater the discrimination. In other words, ableism is one possible answer for a young girl seeing herself as valuable as a princess one week and deflating into shame and self-loathing the next. (Thanks for all you do, *Oxford English Dictionary*, but my definition is better.)

Without using the "ableism" word, I tried to communicate some of this to David. He was nodding along, but I could still feel the chasm between what I know in my blood and my bones and what I'm able to hand him. It's like we grew up right next to the roar of Niagara Falls, but at some point I moved to a cabin in the quiet woods, and now I'm back home, yelling over the noise, trying to explain how overwhelming it is, but David can hardly hear me or the waterfall. What words could I gather to make David feel the rumble surrounding us?

Ableism thunders in the background of every conversation, every story, every building. It's the atmosphere we breathe, a body of principles, rules we live by. We learn its tenets like we learn about good and evil: with subtle and consistent reinforcement. Not only do we avoid questioning them, it doesn't even occur to us that there's anything *to* question. Ableism pushes assumptions like: Some bodies/minds/modes are inherently and always preferable to others. Hearing/speaking is always better than deafness/signing. Bipeds walking is definitively preferable to paraplegics wheeling. Each of us has a "whole," "unmarred," "perfect" body that we were meant to have; the paralyzed, autistic, deaf version is just a sadder, lesser version of that original intent. (This tenet is wrapped up in narratives of fat, aging, gender-nonconforming bodies, too, of course.) The worth of a body is measured by its capacity for work and/or the longevity of life it's able to sustain. Bodies are products; scars, breaks, and changes in function make that product less valuable. Dependence is inferior to independence. Only some bodies require help, and those bodies are a burden. It's only practical to shape the world with the "majority" in mind (and there is such a thing as a majority). Disability is always, only a deficit; the world would be a better place if we could figure out a way to eliminate it entirely. And on and on and on . . .

If you find yourself nodding along with any of these ableist beliefs, that makes sense. They've been a part of our daily diets since infancy. They've made us terrified of aging, wrinkles, belly fat, age spots, sagging skin, and stretch marks. They've turned us into work machines who regularly abuse our bodies to demonstrate our value—sleep less, work harder, always! They've made us ashamed to ask for help, to take medication, to use mobility aids. They stifle our capacity to imagine other ways of being in the world. In order to be okay, we must always strive to be the ideal human: young, smooth, tight, fit, radiant, spry, boundless, unstoppable, independent. Because if we start to spill out of this tiny little mold, what will it mean? Who will we be?

It takes hard work and intention to undo these ideologies. They're loud, insistent, and reinforced at every turn. In fact, the concept of ableism is so deeply entwined with our culture, and, by extension, the wiring of my own self-perception, that sometimes it can be difficult for me to name. I can bend to its insistence just as much as anyone else. Just yesterday I whined to my co-worker about my aging face. "I don't even want to look in the mirror!" I said, covering my face with my hands and making a charming *bleh* sound. Yeah, I'm *not* the picture of post-ableism enlightenment you've been looking for.

Pinpointing the elements that make up an atmosphere of ableism can feel distant and abstract, like knowing the elements that make up oxygen versus knowing what it feels like to breathe in and out. How do I take you through the inhales and exhales?— the way it feels when it's not just a formula in a textbook but an experience that shapes your every day?

Ableism constricts whenever I look for affordable, accessible homes in Kansas City (are there really only three?) or try to navigate the puzzling world of Medicaid in an attempt to keep living. I feel ableism straining my body under the rigidity of inflexible work systems that do not make space for, understand, care for, or believe bodies in pain. I feel the confines of ableism whenever I take the three steps from the driver's seat to the gas pump and forget to breathe in my concentration to make those three steps look as normal and steady as possible, even though it's much easier for me to drag my feet and swing my hips across the same distance. Ableism recommends I put myself through pain and expend extra energy to make sure those strangers walking out of 7-Eleven with a Slurpee don't stare at me, pity me, mock me for the way I move my body.

I wanted David to feel this with me. How do I upload a life of memories, a dictionary of definitions, a planet of feelings? How many times would he need to see people avert their gaze, pull their children back, or fall over themselves to dive fifteen feet out of my way or frantically scramble to open a door lest I attempt to open it myself before he'd know what it means to be both invisible and in the spotlight? At what point would the staring start to make him feel unsteady? How can I take him with me through every grocery store where half of the items tower above my head, every obstacle course sidewalk, each maze between me and the ramp at the back of the building next to the garbage dump, every bar and bank and café with counters so high they erase me from the room, every restaurant and airplane where the toilet is entirely inaccessible to me? Would these field trips illuminate why I started to believe I didn't belong, wasn't welcome, didn't have an invitation to be here? Would it solve the puzzle of a smart, competent girl becoming convinced that she'd never be able to join a workforce that exists on this planet? What hour could he live with me that would give him a glimpse of the power health insurance has over my life?

I ask these questions, not just for David or because I want to understand myself, but because I know I am not the only one who has been relegated to the outside, assigned to the seats designated for Others. So many of us grew up (and continue to exist) under crushing systems—racism, sexism, ageism, classism, homophobia, size discrimination. These structures are like factories pumping out blueprints, designs, infrastructures, tools, and stories that shape our world. They have been running for so long, shaping our cultural history and current landscape, that a lot of us don't even notice the billows of smoke jetting out of their industrial-sized stacks. They are fueled by the worth and power stolen from whole communities. They distort our sense of self, keep us quiet, and make us feel both small and like we're an enormous problem, both invisible and put on display, both a spectacle and swept under the rug.

This act of thievery can be loud and violent, or quiet and sneaky. There are ways these oppressive systems overlap, feed off each other, mirror one another, and there are also ways they remain uniquely distinct. As a white, cis-gendered, straight woman who grew up in a middle-class family, I won't pretend to understand most of these structures intimately. Even in my disabled body, I carry a world of privilege. From where I sit and what I can see, though, shame seems to be a bestselling product pumped out of all of these crushing systems.

So how do we open the eyes of someone already on the inside to what's happening on the outside? Can we trace the ripples well enough to name the larger patterns? As much as numbers put me to sleep, sometimes they capture the scope of the problem in a way a string of observations can't. So here's some data on the United States gathered by Cornell University in 2017: At the time of the study, a person was well over twice as likely to live below the poverty line if they had a disability. The average annual income for a disabled person was $25,400 less than for a nondisabled person. About 80 percent of nondisabled people were employed, compared with 36 percent of disabled people. We could pull many different insights out of these numbers, but one thing is clear: there's a gaping, fundamental disparity between the choices granted to disabled and nondisabled folks.

Then again, numbers catch only so much. Ableism can be hard to hold on to or pinpoint, because it morphs. It lives in distinctly personal stories. It takes on ten thousand shifting faces, and for the world we live in today, it's usually more subtle than overt cruelty. Some examples to start the sketch: the assumption that all people who are deaf would prefer to be hearing—the belief that walking down the aisle at a wedding is obviously preferable to moving down that aisle in a wheelchair—the conviction that listening to an audiobook is automatically inferior to the experience of reading a book with your eyes—the expectation that a nondisabled person who chooses a partner with a disability is necessarily brave, strong, and especially good—the belief that someone who receives a disability check contributes less to our society than the full-time worker—the movie that features a disabled person whose greatest battle is their own body and ultimately teaches the nondisabled protagonist (and audience) how to value their own beautiful life. All of these are different flashes of the same, oppressive structure. Ableism separates, isolates, assumes. It's starved for imagination, creativity, and curiosity. It's fueled by fear. It oppresses. All of us.

When I was small and just learning how to do life in my body, I didn't hesitate, didn't hold back, didn't worry how it would look, didn't look for cues or ask for a line. My imagination ruled. I saw no incongruities in being both a puppy rolling around in the mud and a poised princess. I wore dress-up gowns on afternoon trips to the library and drew magic-marker purple diamonds across my forearms and shins. I didn't wonder what dancing could or should be; I moved my body to music and called it dancing. I used the shelves and cabinets in the kitchen to climb onto the counter, and crawled headfirst down the hardwood stairs at top speed. I scooted around the neighborhood on a red tricycle with streamers flowing out of the handlebars. I was entirely free to *be*, driven by the innovation my body inspired. This is the wild emancipation I wish for all of us—a world where we are all free to be, to move, to exist in our bodies without shame; a world that isn't interested in making all of its humans operate in the exact same way; a world that instead strives to invite more, include more, imagine more. That world sees the humans existing on the margins and says, *You have what we want! What barriers can we remove so we can have you around? What do you need? How can we make that happen?*

"When you grow up in a world that doesn't see you or welcome you or include you or represent you, you believe the world isn't for you," I finally told David. "It's for all the other people." The ones being seen, welcomed, included, represented. This is why I want to unbury the stories, to bring them into the light, to let them breathe in the open air. Because our stories matter. Not only are we a part of this, but we're a vital missing piece.

Thank you for asking, David—and anyone who's reading this book. Even more, thank you for doing your best to listen, even when my words feel unfamiliar or uncomfortable. Here's to building new narrative pathways through our brains, our spaces, our stories. Here's to dismantling ableism, building a bonfire from its pieces, and toasting marshmallows over the flames.

1

AN ORDINARY UNIMAGINABLE LOVE STORY

*I got lost in a Reddit thread recently. As one does. The conver-*sation started with one woman's question for the men of the community: *Would you date a woman who is in a wheelchair?* She wondered because, after eighteen years of using a wheelchair herself, she'd never been in a romantic relationship or on a date. She went on to explain her solid credentials: good sense of humor, sharp and bright, "not ugly." Despite such a winning personality, she suspected her romantic status was a direct result of her disability. She wanted insight from the insiders: *How do I make guys more comfortable with me? How can I be seen as a regular person?*

This woman's question generated 415 comments. As you might imagine, the conversation that ensued is a treasure trove of gems. It includes a collection of cringy wheelchair jokes (if a guy isn't interested, just run over him with your chair!), overt and cloaked ableism (we assume disabled people are nonsexual until told otherwise, so if you want to connect with a guy, you're going to have to learn to tell dirty jokes so we know you're a sexual being), many, many, many questions about sex (no, but REALLY, can you have sex?), blanket oversimplifications (I don't see disability!), and a few earnest attempts to unpack a gut aversion to dating someone in a wheelchair. The most common anxieties, however, were clear: *Will I have to become a caregiver?* and *WHAT. ABOUT. SEX?* Some of my favorite concerns: I worry that she'd make me feel guilty when I go hiking; I don't think I could date a woman in a wheelchair because of all the extra planning it would take to go to the movies; it wouldn't work out, because I have a spiral staircase in my house; I hit on a girl in a wheelchair at a bar one time, and she was nasty to me, so . . .

In the midst of this male-dominated conversation, the single woman who started it all chimed in. I'm pretty sure she replied to each and every comment on this thread, and every time, no matter how ignorant or crass or nonsensical they were, she wrote a thoughtful, charming, diplomatic response. She gave an LOL for their cliché jokes, she soothed their guilt when they confessed their most shallow impulses, she affirmed their gut aversions as normal and understandable. She presented herself as endlessly open-minded, willing to listen, eager to try out their recommendations. She remained flexible, self-assured, playful. I could almost hear her voice—light and warm, putting everyone in the room at ease.

The eeriest bit for me was how much I heard my own voice in her words. The familiarity of relentlessly prioritizing everyone else's comfort over my own took my breath away.

Through her untiring, soothing charm, I started to see it: we're circus performers, riding bikes across tightropes, juggling oranges while singing opera, and we make it look natural, easy. The impossible, relentless task of making other people feel comfortable with our disabilities—of helping them see us as human without making them feel threatened or shamed—is stunningly familiar. The elaborate dance moves required to be accepted by the gang, to get an invitation to the party, to be chosen for the team—the woman on the Reddit thread was an absolute master. The social superpowers she wielded in this conversation reminded me of so many disabled people I know.

Disabled people are expected to cope with their own social ostracism, to handle being misunderstood and misrepresented, and at the same time to put at ease those who perform the ostracism. In order to be seen as equally human, we have to find a way to be seen on the fringes by those already firmly situated on the inside, to make those who would otherwise ignore and erase or misread us feel comfy and cozy and entertained while we attempt to delicately challenge their assumptions.

This dynamic is only heightened when it comes to dating. The task of connecting with another person is layers deep for any human being. But when you add disability into the mix? How do I persuade you I'm human like you? But also, how do I get you to feel comfortable with the ways that I'm different? How do I show you, while maintaining unwavering class, that

I *am* a sexual being? How do I hold all of my own anxieties while also managing yours? How do I flip your ignorance into a joke that educates, entertains, and doesn't make you feel threatened? Meanwhile, for plenty of disabled folks, the stakes couldn't feel higher. For so many, this is the battlefield that rests between here and finding love, partnership, family, a life they want.

Some genuinely insightful comments were sprinkled throughout the Reddit thread. I was struck by the man who had the foresight to recognize that all of us age eventually, and we all become dependent if we live long enough. There was also the man who seemed undaunted by the possible limitations accompanying sex with a paralyzed person. Instead, he saw the unexplored parameter as an opportunity for play. He imagined himself coming up with creative positions, arriving home excited and ready to rearrange the pillows.

These men were the exceptions. The overwhelming impression I had scrolling through the contributions was a tremendous lack of imagination, a reluctance to deviate from some kind of default path and try something different. It was as if they truly believed they knew what they were getting into with a partner they perceived as nondisabled. Somehow, a body that appeared more familiar meant that sex would always go as expected, they would never find themselves in the position of caregiver, their dates would be easy to plan, and they'd always share the same hobbies. They had a picture of love or romance or hooking up or partnership fixed in their minds. Anything outside of that image brought about anxiety, caution, questions. But where did that image even come from? And why are we so fervently wrapped up in it?

* * *

Before almost anything else—before I knew how to read, before I'd figured out how to make my own cup of hot chocolate from a packet of powder, before I had my first best friend—I knew two things: that being loved by a boy was essential, and that love was gained through beauty. Hiding out in our musty basement, I watched hours on hours of my grandmother's taped episodes of *As the World Turns* and learned everything about the mechanics of romance. Sitting frozen on the threadbare burgundy velvet couch, my feet limp and knees scabby from crawling across the wood floors in our house and all over our neighborhood, I watched men crave women's soft, glowing bodies. Women controlled men by tempting them with their easily ripped-open blouses. Whole plotlines twisted and turned on the kind of longing captured in clenched jaws and heavy breathing. I forgot to blink as their bodies spun and tangled with desire. I filed it all away, piecing together what I thought were the rules for everyone.

I saw the same theme everywhere. Muscly men watching nearly nude women dive into the ocean, or women stopping traffic with their long, thin legs walking atop dangerously tall stiletto heels (advertisements for perfume or shaving cream or hamburgers, obviously). So many screens panning women's bodies while boys and men gawked and swooned. In *The Sandlot*

Squints is transformed by the sight of Wendy Peffercorn oiling up on her lifeguard stand, while Chandler and Joey on *Friends* plan their days around watching women in red swimsuits run across the beach on *Baywatch*. There were some variations on the theme, like when the boy beast falls in love with the human girl, or the human boy gawks at the fish girl singing on a rock with her voluptuous red hair flowing; but regardless, the beginning and end of the story revolved around the girl being wanted.

It wasn't all cheap plotlines and confusing advertisements though. Part of my conviction in the importance of being loved by a boy was surely reinforced by the powerful center of my universe—my parents. Their love for each other, particularly my dad's devotion to my mom, felt steadier than the sun's trek across the sky. Every evening at 6:17 he arrived home from his job at the bank in his black suit and tie and went straight to my mom. She'd be in the kitchen making dinner and wearing a real-life apron. She would pause whatever stirring she was doing, and he'd wrap her up in his arms for a good minute. He'd rub his cold ears on her cheek, and she'd scold him, and they'd both grin. I feel like I'm writing a really dull family sitcom right now, but this picture was the backdrop to my days—my suited dad holding my lanky, beautiful blond mother with a spatula in her hand.

Boys infatuated with girls was the plotline of every game of make-believe I played: paper dolls, Barbies, doll house people, and, of course, "house." Acting out scene after scene of tragic car accidents that ended with a doctor falling in love with his (always "his") wounded patient, or a family of sisters who were orphaned, prompting the oldest sister and her boyfriend to become very young, unlikely parents who still managed to find time for steamy make-out scenes. When I finally did get my first best friend, instead of playing queens or cavewomen, we squabbled over who would play the "boy" part. Because what is play without the dramatic conflict of receiving male love and attention?

From Disney and the wobbly VHS recordings of *As the World Turns* to my Barbies and the covers of magazines displayed by the grocery store check-out counter, I had an endless line of images running through my brain. The girls worthy of adoration had itty-bitty waists and dainty little feet, big round boobs below delicate spindle necks. They twirled lightly in a dress, and their mountain of hair bounced back and forth with the smallest turn of the head. Without anyone to tell me otherwise, I identified with this vision. "Yes," I thought. "I choose that."

I believed it was that simple. I saw beauty, and I felt beautiful, so, of course, I surely looked just like the beauty I saw. When I arrived at the inaugural day of sign-language club as a first-grader, we were all asked to come up with our own signed name by choosing a word that described us. "Beautiful," I said. No pause, no doubt, no wavering. I was so confident, I grabbed the whole word for myself. It belonged to me. When I pictured myself, I saw stunning, luminous royalty. I'd twirl my hair through my fingers and see piles of gold. I'd smile and imagine a coy, captivating princess curl on my lips. I'd choose my dress in the morning and could actually see myself in it, graceful and swirling in the wind.

The shoe you are waiting to drop is on its way. Because, of course, I looked nothing like Ariel with her seashell bikini or even Wendy Peffercorn putting lotion on her legs. And while few of us look like a 1990s lifeguard hottie and none of us resembles a cartoon mermaid with eyes the size of fists and a waist the size of a wrist, my body was farther from this ideal than most. It took me longer than you might imagine to realize this. How hard is it to recognize that the clunky leg braces up to your thighs look nothing like the thin, sweeping legs stopping traffic in a lip gloss ad?

I lost my belief in my own beauty in starts and stops, wave after wave of recognition—"Oh, wait! I don't look like that!" And the thought hovering close behind, "I'm *not* beautiful!" It wasn't lost with one misstep and a quick slip from my hand; it was pulled slowly from my clenched fists over the course of years.

When I was fourteen, I went to Lake Michigan with a group of friends. Someone put my hair into two messy buns on top of my head, and I wore a classic black one-piece. Friends took turns giving me piggyback rides to the water; I don't even remember my wheelchair being there. Did we leave it in the car? I spent a lot of the day on a beach towel, rubbing sand between my hands, feeling the sun sink into my shoulders. I felt like Christy Turlington in a Calvin Klein cologne commercial—everything was black and white, organic, flawless, slow motion, while Aimee Mann sang softly in the background, "What the world needs now is love sweet love." About a month later, I saw video footage someone had recorded of the afternoon. Watching the clip took my breath away—a stab in the gut—I was horrified. What I saw was so far from Christy Turlington in black and white; my torso was thick and twisted, my shoulders were broad in contrast to my limp and flabby legs, my feet looked like I was wearing heavy gray booties. I could barely stand to keep my eyes on the footage. It was gruesome to me.

Again and again, I felt jarred when the image captured in the frame didn't look anything like those visions of beauty I'd gathered within me—thin, delicate, dainty, unscarred, unmarred, unbound. My actual appearance matched much sadder images I'd seen—I looked more like something medical, tragic, painful, broken. That wasn't who I wanted to be, or even who I felt my-self to be. I started to crop my lower half out of every image. If I never saw it, I could pretend it didn't exist.

Even when shame wasn't the loudest voice in my head, there was this practical piece to passion and desire that I couldn't work through. As early as fifth grade, I'd sit on my bed and try to work it out in my diary. How would it go? What would it look like for a guy to ravish me? To want me? In *As the World Turns* guys pushed women up against walls or slowly, gently lowered them onto beds and couches and mossy forest floors. Part of it was the mechanics of the thing—would he have to help me undress? Would he have to lift me out of my chair? (Neither option sounds bad now, but at the time, such prospects mortified me.) But it wasn't just the sex. I couldn't even picture a romance between a paralyzed person and a standing partner. How would these two hug? Walk down the street together? Dance? Pose for photos? I had never seen it. I found myself with a lack of imagination on a par with our Favorite Men of Reddit. If we've never seen it, is it even possible?

No one ever said the words, but I pieced them together on my own, slowly, methodically, and over time: "You are too grotesque to be wanted. You don't belong in a love story." I carried this lump in my belly, and it pumped toxins to my limbs and up my spine on the daily.

When I did allow myself to fantasize, I did so by playing one enormous trick on my brain: in my fantasies, I was always a nondisabled version of myself. My body was symmetrical, with working legs. My feet were dainty and pink. My waist was so very thin, and I moved through every space with grace and ease.

✳ ✳ ✳

Sam Wagner was my one chance—at a love story, at being loved, at living the life of a wife. He was the youngest boy in a family of seven kids all born within the span of eight years. We went to church with the Wagners, and when Sam and I were eight years old, he spent all of his allowance money to buy me a $3.95 Magic Eye book I'd picked out of my school's Scholastic catalogue. His generous gift set off a tiny spark that maybe, if I wished it into the universe with all of my whole earnest heart, Sam would love me enough to marry me one day.

For years, I saw Sam once a week at Sunday school. I'd wear my prettiest Sunday dresses, have my mom curl my hair with hot curlers that singed my forehead and the edges of my ears, and sit silently through church trying to see whether Sam no-

ticed how pretty I looked. Maybe he'd glance over in my direction when the boys teased the girls during Bible Trivia, but most
weeks he seemed to have forgotten the flash of special closeness
we'd felt when we were just a bit smaller. The rest of the week, I
pined. I started praying each night on a bright star, then wishing
every night at 11:11 for this unfathomable dream to come true.
(When willing a miracle into the world, it's important to cover
all your bases.) In the meantime, I started telling everyone who
cared to listen (and some who didn't) that I didn't want to get
married when I grew up. I proclaimed the business to be a dis-
tasteful one. Because, if you *decide* to become an Old Maid, it's
one hundred times less pathetic than if you're forced into Old
Maidenhood against your will.

I still don't know what did the trick—probably the hot
curlers—but slowly, slowly, as the years stretched out and we
turned into adolescents, Sam really did start to pay attention
to me. He'd sit near me on the bus during youth group trips,
and we'd sing along loudly to Relient K. He'd ask me and a
handful of other church kids over to his house "to sing praise
and worship songs," then ask to braid my hair as we sat around
the fire pit in his backyard. I believed myself so rigidly stuck
in my disabled role outside of love stories that it was very difficult for me to believe Sam saw me as anything other than his
nonthreatening gal pal. I didn't truly believe he felt anything
special toward me until one 2 a.m. phone call, me sitting on the
kitchen floor and Sam hiding in his basement, when he said
the words, "I'm really into you."

"Really?" I said. I could hardly wrap my head around it. This was some kind of wire-crossing, slipping-through-the-cracks fluke, and I treasured the miracle.

I knew people watched us and didn't quite know what to think. There were no couples that looked like us in any mainstream spaces. Except maybe Christopher and Dana Reeve, but they'd been married before the accident that brought tragedy to their marriage. Their relationship wasn't a model of sexy chemistry or appealing intimacy; it was the image of the desperate quest for a cure to right an obvious wrong. If Sam and I were to have our romance depicted on-screen, we would be in a comedy where everyone laughed at the cringy "handicapped" girl who thought she had a real chance at love (think Joan Cusack in *Sixteen Candles* trapped in headgear trying to drink out of a water fountain or talk to a boy on the bus) or in a painful, tear-jerking flick about the selfless hero who's able to look beyond the grotesque deformities and love the broken girl, despite (think *A Walk to Remember*, but replace the exquisite dying Mandy Moore with the image of a freakish version of Joan Cusack trapped in headgear, etc.).

When people saw Sam and me together, they placed us in one of two stories—the embarrassing comedy spectacle or the breathtaking picture of the truest love on the planet. This stood in stark contrast to the real story about two teenagers who liked each other.

In my experience of love, high school boys might be tied for first with our Favorite Men of Reddit in their reluctance to imagine. I felt the discomfort from Sam's school friends. They were more likely to place our romance into some kind of absurd comedy worth cheap, thoughtless laughs. I still remember hearing about the guy in his class who teased Sam, saying, "At least my girlfriend can run." I read the words now, and they have the sting of one sad, crumpled red cup—it's empty and weak. *Yay for you! A girlfriend who runs! Sounds like a great time. You must be so happy together, what with the running she does.* Even Sam didn't seem too bothered by the joke at the time. But I remember turning the sentence over and over in my head—*at least my girlfriend can run*. Because, of course, it tapped into so much more than just running. Girls who run are the girls worth catching. They use their running skills to twirl and walk down runways and have all the fun in bed. Girls who can't run might as well be old ladies living in nursing homes that smell stale and sad.

The "breathtaking romance" was a more common narrative attached to us, and it was not an appealing alternative. I became accustomed to older women at our church stooping down to my ear, uncomfortably close to my face, and fervently whispering that I was so lucky to be loved by such a man. *Can you believe how much that young man loves her?* they'd ask each other. *Amazing.*

I could never forget how lucky I was to be loved by Sam. Which made the experience of dating him very confusing. Because, it turns out, I didn't actually like him the way I thought I did. I mean, yes, I liked him. Especially at first. But very quickly my crush turned into a begrudging affection, like the way you care for a little brother who grates on your every nerve, but he's been through a lot of life with you and also, he's pretty cute when he falls asleep on a road trip, so you can't just throw him out on big trash day. At the same time, you probably wouldn't choose your obnoxious little brother, or even his equivalent, to partner with for life. I'd known Sam since we were eight years old. I loved the way he romped through the snow like a puppy and loved me with the same thoughtless loyalty. A love I was sure I didn't deserve. But the way he couldn't stop jiggling his leg or whistling through his teeth drove me up the wall. And more than the tics and the noise, there was something else. I didn't know what it was—I'd never been with any other person, so it was difficult to put my finger on—but it felt something like being invisible. I could say or do anything—shout, throw a fit, jump on the roof, burn down the house—and Sam would look at me in the same exact way. Did he see me at all?

We talked about breaking up about once a month. I'd reach a breaking point—*Why am I with this person? I don't even LIKE him!* Sam would always talk me down—*Love is sacrifice! If this were easy, something would be wrong.* We talked about it over and over again, but in the end, the conversations started to feel more like gestures. Childish fits. The idea of breaking up with Sam never really felt possible, because I knew what it meant. If I ended things with this harmless man-child, I would be alone for the rest of my life. I would never have a family of my own. Never feel loved again. Never feel wanted. And choosing to give all that up felt foolish. I could put up with almost anything to avoid being alone and unwanted.

I remember the moment when I realized I'd never actually break up with him. I looked at my face in the mirror—this face with a long nose, tiny lips, and tired eyes—and told myself to be honest. Realistic. This was it. I couldn't imagine any other path for the girl in the wheelchair.

At the wise age of twenty-two, we decided to get married.

✳ ✳ ✳

I was a bridesmaid four times before I was a bride. With each wedding my disabled bridesmaid body required rearrangements and cringy adaptations, especially in the perfectly posed group wedding photos. *Now, all of the bridesmaids stand on a different stair and circle the bride. And what should we do with the one who doesn't stand . . . hmm . . . have her sit on the floor? Yes, good thinking.* The older I got, the more I felt like the aesthetic failure of other people's weddings—the object that did not belong, the weird outsider who threw off their pictures, the person whose body would not cooperate with the most accommodating of dresses. Weddings were supposed to be pretty enough for the cover of a magazine, and it seemed like the disabled bridesmaid threw the whole wedding off course.

When it was time for me to be a bride, I was adamant that I walk down the aisle. In the months approaching my wedding with Sam, I started practicing with a physical therapist. She'd call over an extra hand to carry a full-length mirror in front of me so I could watch myself as I took steps with a walker, paying attention to the sight of my hips (one fell lower, while the other did the work of two), my feet (one always dragging behind), even my arms (with veins that bulged like a bodybuilder under the strain, which mortified me). I looked awkward, clunky, rough, haggard. Nothing like the dainty floating brides I had in my head. I gripped the handlebars of my walker, tried to remember to breathe, and put all of my brain power into lifting that right foot, lifting that left hip. Too soon, my forehead would dampen, my wrists would start to tremble under the effort.

At the time, I had no idea that my drive to walk down the aisle was such an established trope. Paralyzed brides (and grooms) getting out of their wheelchairs and walking down aisles is an entire genre of YouTube videos. Do the people who make and watch these videos know how ubiquitous they are? Even more pressing to me, have they put any energy into questioning why these videos are so popular? Why viewers relish them? Why so many brides feel the need to push themselves so very hard just to avoid using a mobility aid during an exchange of vows? Why brides believe it's infinitely better if they don't have mobility aids with them when they commit to joining their lives with another person?

On the surface, these videos fulfill the requirements of our favorite triumph-over-adversity stories. *Yay! It feels good when someone defies a prognosis, jumps over an obstacle, accomplishes a hard-earned goal.* But other stories are being reinforced here, too. Brides and wheelchairs are among the most rigidly fixed symbols in our collective stories. Brides walking down aisles are symbols of purity and goodness and beauty; we see them as the promise of the beginning of life. Mobility aids are sad symbols of defeat and disease; we see them as the promise of old age, the end. The mixing of these two symbols unsettles.

Runaway Bride came out when I was thirteen. It was THE sleepover movie. We'd line up our sleeping bags, pull out our knitting (that's right, we were the cool thirteen-year-olds in your class), and act out all of Julia Roberts's lines with her (as we said it, "You wouldn't know love if it bit you in the ARMPIT!"). During my adolescence, this movie was one of many favorites, as was *My Best Friend's Wedding* (1997), *The Wedding Singer* (1998), *The Wedding Planner* (2001), and *My Big Fat Greek Wedding* (2002), all of which include brides who stand and walk and wear long puffy dresses that are put on prime display during the essential walking-down-the-aisle scene. Countless stories, endless scenes to reinforce two fixtures: (1) The most important story for a girl is getting married, and (2) getting married isn't for disabled girls (or queer girls, or fat girls, or older girls, and, unless you're JLo, it would seem it's not for girls of color, either).

I didn't know how to picture myself wheeling down the aisle without the scene making me cringe. I felt like an imposter, trying to fool people into believing that I, too, was a pretty girl someone would want to marry. I left my wheelchair outside the doors of the sanctuary and wouldn't even allow the support of a walker or a crutch to tamper with this scene; instead, I held on to my mom and dad as they helped me walk down the aisle toward Sam. If you didn't know any better, you might just have seen me as a regular bride, pretty and perfect and pure. The music was dramatic, and the pews were filled with six hundred faces watching me take one step after another. I knew it was an important moment. When I think about it now, though, I don't remember the grip of my parents' hands or Sam's face at the end of the aisle. I don't even remember the labor of lifting each foot. I just remember feeling detached from myself, out of my body, watching the scene from above. Just like a movie, I wasn't actually there.

✳ ✳ ✳

As you probably have guessed, the marriage didn't go well. Turns out trying to partner up with your obnoxious little brother is not a sustainable gig. The brutality of being married to a person you've chosen out of fear and convenience was a fast lesson in realizing that being partnered with just anyone is not the end-all, be-all setup I'd always imagined. Being loved by a boy can actually be a real-life nightmare. In fact, being entirely alone could be exponentially better—more fulfilling and satisfying and exciting—than being partnered with the wrong person.

Out of desperation to get out, I found myself boldly unafraid of solitude, independence, or even being undesirable to potential love interests. What I found in this fearlessness was delicious: Nights alone drinking red wine and chomping down whole bowls of popcorn with Angela Lansbury on *Murder, She Wrote*. Sleeping in late with purring orange cats circling the top of my head. Reading every Jane Austen novel with hot drinks clumsily concocted from my sputtering, thrifted espresso maker. I leaned heavily into this sacred solitude for years.

Once I realized I was happy alone, there was a comfort in keeping it that way. I didn't go on dates much. I was more the type to develop a crush on a person I barely knew, read every social media post they'd ever made, and finally, after months of truly unattractive obsessing, send them a random, easy-breezy message with the secret hope that they would respond with a declaration of love. Because, after all of that silent pining, HOW COULD THEY NOT?

I finally started an online dating account because (1) my roommate got a serious boyfriend, and the pair of them seemed very invested in getting me a boyfriend of my own, and (2) I was curious. So much of my rationale on dating and relationships had developed entirely in my head. I had one shitshow of an experience, and the rest had played out on screens and in magazines and was twisted into something defeating and excruciating. At the empowering age of twenty-eight, I wanted to see: Would a wheelchair really be a giant obstacle for people? Would I put all this thought into my online profile and hear crickets in response? Or worse, would men be cruel? Would they laugh at me? Would they fetishize me? I was prepared for some uncomfortable dates that would make for great stories I could later recount for the entertainment of my best pals. I was even prepared for getting hurt. I wouldn't let myself hope for much more than that.

I'm pretty sure I put more time and energy into curating my profile than any other online dating citizen. I agonized over which pictures to use, trying to find just the right number that included my disability, but to just the right proportion. What handful of images could convey that disability was a part of me without eclipsing all of me? How could I emphasize that I loved my nieces and nephews and eating take-out on porches and my own funky style without pretending that my paralyzed body wasn't a part of all of it? How could I invite people to really see me without scaring them off?

In the box designated for additional information about me, I wrote: "The wheelchair thing gives me a unique perspective on life, and it doesn't slow me down much—I drive a truck and love hanging out with my friends around the city. I value my independence, but also appreciate the relationships I have where I feel safe/close enough to accept help from time to time. It's not awkward for me at all if you have any questions about this part of me. What else . . . ? I think the most beautiful things are found in improbable places and the most mundane moments can also be miraculous. I value authenticity and originality. I think it's important to always strive to be a kinder, more compassionate, and generous person." I pondered over every word, every tone and shade.

I realized very quickly that few men had put a quarter of the thought into their profiles. In fact, I'm not sure how many men who contacted me had even glanced at my carefully crafted page long enough to see the wheelchair in two of the eight images.

At first I was pretty bored with the whole dance. There was the older guy with kids who only ever sent me long, quippy messages about how ordinary his life was. I found myself wondering what it might be like to be someone's stepmom, but the messages slowed, and I hardly noticed. There was the sweetie pie in the blue baseball cap who met me for ice cream on a Saturday afternoon and clearly didn't know what to do with a first date who asked follow-up questions after every little life detail he shared:

"And then my parents got divorced, and I went to live with my mom . . ."

"What was that like?"

"Fine? Okay. I guess?"

"Really. It was 'fine'?"

"Yeah. So anyways . . ."

That guy continued to send me dragon pun memes for weeks after our date, which still mystifies me. I liked the dragon pun memes. I didn't like one-word answers to my prodding questions. We didn't go on a second date.

Then there was the heavily cologned fellow who didn't say a word about my wheelchair until I brought it up more than an hour into our dinner. When I asked him what it meant to him that I had a disability, he deflected and minimized without missing a beat. "It's not like it defines you," he said. To be fair, what an awful question to pose to a person on a first date. Out of the blue, BAM. *Go!* Also, how interesting to have this guy across the table define for me the place that disability had in my own life. I don't remember what I said, but in my fantasy life, it was heavy with sarcasm: *Ooooh! That's the role disability plays in my life! I'd been hoping someone would tell me.*

My forever favorite interaction from online dating was with the scientist—a problem-solver, finding his great riddle in the disabled woman he'd met online! Really, I should have stopped messaging this guy as soon as he started educating me on my profession teaching English (a profession that he did not share.

Not even close, Mr. Science Guy). I knew this was going nowhere fast. But I was also very curious. What else might this
man have to teach me? Soon I discovered he had a plan for
curing my paralysis. It turns out, he had transformed his experience of type 1 diabetes through a very specific diet (which might
make some sense?—I wouldn't know), and he was convinced
that my ailments could also be solved, at least partially, through
a similar regimen (which makes no sense, and I would know).
We'd probably have to add some exercises to the routine, but, as
he assured me, he'd figure it out.

After a month of these fun times, I was amused, but little more.
I had not felt a single spark of connection—in fact, nothing that
even approximated a sizzle. I felt like an odd duck. Not necessarily because of the wheelchair in my dating profile pictures, but
because something about the way I saw the world didn't match
these people I'd met. Was it the wheelchair that had shaped that
lens? Surely in part, right? Mixed with being the youngest of six in
a family fueled by feelings and storytelling and the understanding
that we had no money all with a backdrop of chemotherapy and
surgeries and braces on my legs under the glow of the Midwest
in the 1980s and 1990s. All of it, forces at work shaping me into
the person who just couldn't brush by life's painful or complicated
bits. *My parents' divorce was fine. Disability doesn't define me. The
paralysis can be fixed.* None of it was traumatic. It just didn't make
my eyes dance.

This confirmed what I'd been thinking for a while, but this
time, it didn't feel as ominous. My story probably wouldn't include romance. I wasn't a good fit for partnering with another

person. And truly, that was okay with me. I liked my story as it was. I liked who I was on my own. This was a hard-earned space I'd created for myself, and I was grateful to rest there.

And then, one measly month into the online dating, there was Micah. I found his face while scrolling through pages of profile pictures with my mom, giggling at all the shirtless, bathroom-mirror selfies. We both paused over his charming half grin. He wasn't in a bathroom, no mirrors were in sight, and he was wearing a shirt!

"Send him a smiley face!" my mom demanded. She was giddy over his half smile.

"Hold on," I said, grinning back at his photo. "Let's just see about this Micah, 28." As I scrolled through his profile, I felt tiny little lovebirds flapping around my head. First, he knew how to write a sentence, including the proper use of a comma between two independent clauses connected by a conjunction, which was pretty much a seduction dance in my book. The more I read, the more I marveled. Was this a real person? Had the internet created him out of a lifetime collection of my Google searches and online shopping? This guy valued story-telling, curiosity, and artistic expression. He liked one-on-one conversations and was looking for someone who would be easy to talk to (Ding! Ding! Ding!). And, the real clincher, he made a joke reference to *Dr. Quinn, Medicine Woman*. Hello, you may have my heart right here and now, really, here it is, it's yours. I sent him a smiley face.

By the time I'd gotten in my car for the drive home, Micah had sent one back. I learned only later that we almost missed that connection. He had three weeks left on his subscription to the dating site and hadn't checked his account for messages in months. Fifteen minutes after I sent the little smiley face, he had gotten back on. He thought the smiley face had been waiting for weeks. For all he knew, it had been. I like this detail in the story. It's the sprinkle of serendipitous in a digital romance constructed by algorithms. We sent messages back and forth into the night.

Actually, we sent messages back and forth through the month of September. Messages about birth order, both being the spoiled, angsty youngests, and how much we essentially idolized our older siblings. We each praised the other for pursuing an impractical, soul-nourishing degree in college, talked about our childhood connections to C. S. Lewis and Roald Dahl, and argued over the merits of Team Peeta versus Team Gale. (Team Peeta all the way, obviously.) As our messages expanded, they deepened. We talked about longing and grief, suffering and joy, deconstructing and reconstructing our personal beliefs about faith and church and religion. It wasn't until two weeks in, on September 13, that Micah asked me about my wheelchair. Gracefully, with care and curiosity in the middle of a back-and-forth thread about pain and empathy, he wrote: "You mention in your profile that you've used a walker and a chair since you were young. Is that something that has taught you empathy? How has it shaped your life? Maybe it's a ridiculous request, asking you to fit such a large matter into a typed message, and maybe there's a more polite way to be curious about such a situation, but curious I am, and so I ask."

His question, his tone, his word choice delighted me. I treasured his genuine curiosity. Not a greedy grab for gory details, but humble interest. An acknowledgment that he didn't know what it meant to me, and he wasn't about to step in and try to fix anything. He simply extended an invitation for me to share my stories. I couldn't have crafted the inquiry better myself.

We spent our first date eating giant cookies dipped in big mugs of coffee on a Wednesday night. When I coasted up the ramp to meet him, I don't remember thinking about how he saw me—what the image of my paralyzed body sitting in a wheelchair might mean to him. Why is that? Maybe, in that moment when I saw him sitting alone on the patio of the coffee shop, I trusted that I was already so much more complicated to him than just one wheelchair or one turquoise dress with a lace collar (which is what I'd chosen to wear after three hours of deliberation). I rolled my hands into a pretend telescope (like I was a pirate sighting him across the ocean?) and said, "It's you! You're a real person!" We sat under a red umbrella, and I started talking too much, too fast, and he smiled and bobbed his head and chuckled sweetly. Hours passed, I calmed down, and we hadn't even begun to run out of things to tell and ask each other. Even when it started pouring rain, we huddled closer under our red umbrella and giggled at just how wild the storm was getting—were those actual rivers of water rushing down the street behind us?

Our first date was sweet and perfect. Then we had some weird ones. Like the moment during the second date when he told me he'd been a real heartbreaker in high school, and I sort of gagged in my own mouth and decided that I probably couldn't ever love him. Because who attracts endless love interest in high school of all times? People I can't identify with. Or our third date, when he invited me over to hang out with his roommates to watch *Hot Rod*, and I glared at the TV the entire time. Because (1) I kind of hate movies where you're supposed to laugh when the characters crash or get smashed by heavy moving objects, and (2) Micah's roommates were great and all, but I didn't really want to hang out with Micah's roommates.

On one of those early dates, we went thrift store shopping, and Micah confessed he didn't know how to walk with me. "Do I walk behind you? Do I rest my hand on your handlebar?" I didn't know what to tell him, but I liked that he let me in on his uncertainty. "I don't know, how does this feel?" I asked, grabbing his hand and dragging him up the aisle. At first he didn't want to push me anywhere. To him, it felt aggressive, controlling—the opposite of his driving force. "To *me*, it sort of feels like we're holding hands," I said. He considered. He hadn't thought of it that way before. And bit by bit, we created our own currency, our own intimacies, our personalized displays of affection. From scratch, we imagined our love to life. Micah pushed my chair by slipping his hands behind my back. He kissed the top of my head while we moved down the street. I rested the back of my head on his forearm. He lifted me out of my chair and into the car to avoid the puddle by the passenger door. I gave him rapid-fire kisses on his cheek and committed his smile wrinkles to memory.

I was sure Micah was worried about sex, but he didn't bring

it up. In my head, fears about sex was the #1 reason nondisabled people didn't ask out disabled people. That was definitely on my radar, and I hadn't even been on Reddit yet. I felt an urgency to soothe any fears he might be keeping close to his chest, so one afternoon, sitting on my orange couch under the frosty window, I asked. "Do you have any questions about sex?"

Micah was casual and calm. "I actually read a few blogs and a really helpful article about sex and paralysis."

"Did you?" I asked, amused and delighted. How simple, how helpful, how smart!

"Yeah, I mean, I felt a little silly, because they all basically said, 'Of course disabled people can have sex.'"

I beamed at this curious, intelligent person I'd picked to sit with me on my orange couch, to introduce to my cranky cats, to spend all of my Saturdays with. He made the unimaginable love story feel so ordinary.

A couple of years after Micah and I had been together, I went to his winter work party with him. Earlier that month I had passed the comprehensive exams for my PhD program, which felt like an enormous feat, and I had just buzzed my hair as a sort of empowering celebration. I was feeling in the prime of my radiance and strength. Micah and I were happy together, and I felt particularly beautiful with my recently shorn head. I entered that party feeling valuable. Two gin and tonics in and I was having a blast, meeting Micah's co-workers, putting faces to stories. The hall was dimly lit, and a buzz of energy was running through the room.

We'd been in a conversation with one of his co-workers for

a good bit, listening to him talk about his time in seminary and the online courses he was currently taking. I was genuinely interested, asking all of the follow-up questions, like I do, when the guy took a quick detour and started asking how Micah and I met. Did I mention to him how vulnerable I had felt dating online with a disability? I don't know what prompted the next part of the conversation, but even before I recognized what was happening, I started to feel the room disintegrate around me. "I just really commend you, man," the co-worker said to Micah. At first, we were both confused. Our nodding slowed, our faces scrunched just a bit. Why did Micah deserve praise? "For dating her," the co-worker clarified. "A lot of guys wouldn't even look at that profile. That says a lot about you." I heard myself wholeheartedly agreeing. "Yeah, he's a special one!" I shouted up at the man who'd just made me feel so small, giving Micah a little punch in the bicep. Chuckle, chuckle, chuckle. I continued smiling and chatting all night, all the while wanting to disappear. I felt so foolish, showing up to this party with confidence, assuming Micah's co-workers would see me as anything more than evidence of his benevolence.

As the night went on, I drank more gin and tonics, and by the time Micah and I were making our way to the parking lot, I had found my indignation. I rehearsed for Micah the tongue-lashing I should have given his small-minded co-worker, and that night in my diary, I drunkenly wrote: "to the little toad who wanted to give bonus points for dating a girl in a wheelchair: fuck you, you tiny dick-rag in the back of a dirty drain with sick-ass fish. Fuck you." I'm not exactly sure of the precise image this insult is supposed to call forth, or what sick-ass fish have to do with any of it. But what strikes me here is twofold: (1) the sting of his ignorance still cut me deep, even after years of unpacking my disability, coming into my own, finding genuine love, and growing in self-worth. With four swift sentences, he still possessed the power to completely undo me. And (2) I no longer saw myself as the sole source of the problem. With an hour and a splash of alcohol, I moved through my own self-loathing to locate the problem outside of myself. And even if I hadn't figured out how to navigate that shift yet—even if I handled it with rage and a filthy mouth—it was a step away from making my body a perfect host for shame. I was able to recognize that this guy lacked understanding. That he could imagine only the stories he'd already been told, and in those stories, disability was only ever linked to sad defects, broken bodies, and dashed hopes.

When I think about our Favorite Men of Reddit and their response to the question "Would you date a woman in a wheelchair?," I'm struck by the unfortunate, unnecessary barriers seeping through so many responses. *I just can't imagine how it would work.* What a tiny planet to create for yourself. What a limited way to experience love, intimacy, sexuality, partnership, and play. *If I haven't seen it, is it even possible?* Of course it is. You have the power to create, to imagine, to build and rebuild. There are so many more stories waiting to be written.

Instead of disability as the limitation, what if a lack of imagination was the actual barrier? It's our affinity for familiarity that traps us. Our impulse to adhere to that which came before. To stick with the script, follow instructions, keep with the norms. I think the assumption is that this will keep us safe. But the truth is, of course, that we are never safe. On the surface it sounds bleak, I know, but there is something liberating here, too. Thrilling. Inspiring. Anytime we open up our hearts to another person, we risk it all, and keeping our hearts closed is the most straightforward guarantee for loss.

I was much quicker to know that I wanted Micah in my life for the long haul. He took a little longer, and that stung. It also felt true to his careful approach to life, and probably a bit more reasonable than my flash, bang, boom approach. But even after we both felt comfortable using the word "forever" with each other, we weren't settled on the choice to get married. For me, marriage was wrapped up in the default route to life. I'd been there and had jumped out as quickly as the law allowed. Getting married meant an ostentatious wedding where I didn't feel present or real—it was trying to fit into a role I'd seen play out countless times in stories that didn't represent me. How could I hold on to my distinct self under a structure as powerful and loud and established as marriage?

At the same time, I felt myself longing for a ritual, a day to mark, a ceremony with witnesses, a pocket in time and space to set down intentions with this miraculous, ordinary person I liked the most. Was there a way to build our own structure? To reimagine what two people can be to each other? To wipe the slate clean and create something from scratch? Did we have to do this thing like anyone we'd seen before, or could we use our unique quirks and rhythms as the guide?

In some ways, I think my disability is the force that disassembled the template to begin with. Then I found a person who already wanted something different, too. From the way our bodies reach for each other to the expectations we have for the future, we are open and curious. Together, we used our blank slate as an invitation for play and imagination.

I didn't want a flashy ring or a one-way proposal. We chose a day to mutually recognize what the other person meant to us and declare our intention to commit to a very large building project together. We made collage wedding invitation zines using magazine clippings and thread. We invited only our families—the people who had known us since we were fresh and small and would still be there when we were wrinkled.

There was no aisle at our ceremony, and I definitely didn't walk anywhere. My chair was a part of all the photos, an extension of me, a part of our romance. My dress was short, form-fitting, and all lace. (I also bought it for $7 at a thrift store three days before the ceremony.) Micah wore a pink floral short-sleeve button-up with a lavender tie, and we rented the rooftop of a building on the edge of downtown. We asked two of our favorite friends, Alyssa and Maren, to officiate, my sister to speak good words around us, and Micah's sister to say a blessing. We all sat in a circle as the sun went down. Micah and I wrote a song together that we sang at the ceremony. It's kind of like a vow song, but mostly a reminder of why we chose each other. A song to get in our heads, to sing in the shower or while we're cooking or when we've forgotten why we're together. A song to come back to us year after year.

Yesterday morning I slept in later than Micah. I'm always

sleepier than he is, and on weekends, he gets up first and feeds the crying cats or washes the dishes that have inevitably piled up throughout the week. I rolled out of our bedroom in a giant sweatshirt with my big wooly socks and my bangs sticking straight up like an eighties rocker. I found him working on the computer in our study. Our cranky orange cats were snuggling on the couch behind him, and the rain was making padding noises on our windows. I reached my arms out for him. He moved over to me and climbed onto my lap, straddling me. This is not a scene that has been choreographed in any love story that I've ever seen—rom com, drama, or otherwise—but I nestled into his chest, breathed in his scent, and felt the muscle ropes along his back. (And somewhere out in the world, the tiny minds of Our Favorite Men of Reddit simultaneously exploded.) This was our space, our story, our love. I rested there for a good moment and savored us.

3

MORE THAN A DEFECT

"Today we're going to talk about two models of disability—the medical model and the social model." I'm talking loudly, pronouncing each word with precision and care, and using my hands to push invisible ideas through the air as a group of high school seniors find places for their backpacks, lean back in their chairs, and whisper loudly to each other about whatever important events happened since they saw each other a few hours ago. I try to signal that we're getting started by ignoring the buzz and diving in.

Sitting in my wheelchair, I'm at eye level with them, and some have to crane their necks to see me as I push myself back and forth in front of the class. "When I talk about models of disability," I say, "I want you to imagine that each model is like a different set of glasses you put on." I place an imaginary set of spectacles on the bridge of my nose. "One set of lenses draws out a particular set of details, while the other set reveals something entirely different."

During my time in graduate school, I'd given a handful of lectures and presentations on these ideas to college students and academic peers, but this is my first time teaching high schoolers, my first time teaching a disability-focused class, my first time seeing a group of kids five days a week as we work through this material. One month after I defended my dissertation on disability studies and creative nonfiction, I took this job teaching English at an independent high school. I hadn't been in a high school classroom since I was a student in one, well over a decade before, and I'd never been a student in a high school that expected as much from its students. I was recklessly breaking the unspoken rules of the community (don't assign seniors a paper so close to their college application deadlines, don't write page-long comments on report cards, don't take it personally) and the silent, consistently reinforced values (succeeding, winning, perfecting, more, higher, better, best!).

Instead, my headspace was entirely wrapped up in the work I'd devoted myself to over the previous three years—reading and breathing, writing and dreaming about disability theory, working with texts that felt as supernaturally powerful to me as the Bible had when I was a fervent teenager. By the time I graduated, I saw myself as the chosen disciple who would go forth and teach the people the Truth I'd been given. I was confident that the rampant ableism I felt coursing through the world would be remedied rather simply through education. The problem was just that people hadn't received a clear presentation of the right information. And wouldn't you know—I *had* that information! We were so close to revelation.

One of the greatest appeals of the job was the ability to design my very own semester course for the seniors. I spent the rest of the summer dreaming it up—"Cripples, Freaks, and Invalids: The Marginalized Body as Seen in the Stories We Tell." I marveled at my great luck in finding a job where I could fulfill my purpose so directly. I agonized over cuts to the reading list and crafted the perfect activities that would allow my future students to really experience the content of the course. I was a bit intimidated to teach this particular group of teenagers. Our school was known for producing the very highest standardized test scores and sending its students off to all of the Ivy Leagues. I worried that they'd chew through disability studies too quickly—that I'd run out of ideas for them to think through.

"So, the medical model and the social model: two sets of lenses that show you the same scene in different ways. One lens, the medical model, is the default set. This is the way we typically look at disability—the way we've looked at disability for a really long time. When you see through this lens, you immediately see the disabled body as a problem that needs to be fixed." I click to a slide with a rough sketch of a woman in a wheelchair sitting at the bottom of a flight of stairs. She looks haggard and frazzled. Her hair is a bit of a mess. In the back of my mind, I wonder whether my students see me in this image—helpless, powerless, ineffectual—but I don't have time to reflect on it. This isn't about me; this is about giving them some new ideas to try on.

"Approached using the medical model, this woman and her

wheelchair are the only problem that needs fixing. This perspective fixates on the deficiencies in the individual. Maybe there's a cure for her legs. Maybe we can figure out a way to get her upright so she can walk up those stairs. Or maybe she should just try to find another building." I slap my hand against her illustrated legs, my own paralyzed ones resting beneath hers on my wheelchair's footplate. This explanation seems to make easy sense to them. The medical model feels obvious. What other way is there to look at it?

"But the social model sees this scene differently," I explain, excited to share the big reveal, a shift in perspective that had changed everything for me. "Instead of fixating on *disability* as The Problem, the social model focuses on the *experience* of disability, the *context* of disability, the *environments* creating disabling moments. The social model looks at this image and says, 'Let's shift our focus from the woman in the wheelchair to the building with only one point of access. How limiting!' The social model says, 'Let's build a ramp! An elevator! Let's redesign this building with fewer stairs, and while we're at it, let's open up this floor plan!'" I'm practically singing this part of the lecture, having a dance party in my own head, skipping rapidly over ideas that have lived in my limbs and shaped all of my disabled days for the past three decades. *Isn't this fun? Isn't this life-changing?!*

In the middle of my euphoria, I glance back at my students. The vibe of the entire group seems to have shifted without my noticing. I see squinted eyes, blank faces, scrunched brows. Some of them look entirely skeptical. My heart starts racing, so I talk faster. I hadn't wanted to bring myself into this, but I'm scrambling for something that will make these ideas feel tangible to them. I reach for a simple example from my life and pick out only the most basic facts. "Okay, so, for example: When I arrive at school, I'm able to push a button that opens the door, I ride an elevator to the third floor and enter this room, no problem. I have complete access to the spaces I need to enter. What could have been a 'disabling experience'—the inability to enter a building— has been remedied in this case." They continue to stare back at me with no visible evidence of understanding. "Does that make sense?" I ask, trying to sound casual, hoping they're just hiding all signs of comprehension.

"Yeah . . . but. The disability is still there. It's not like it just disappears," one boy says. I notice how he avoids linking me to the disability itself. I picture the disembodied "disability" hovering somewhere above me, then diving off to haunt some other unsuspecting body.

"I see what you're saying." I nod vigorously, wanting so much to affirm any attempt to engage these ideas. "What's your name again?" I'm still getting to know these kids, still trying to keep all the floppy-haired boys straight in my head.

"Adam," he says.

"Adam! That's right." Star of the soccer team, Adam. Drives a shiny new sports car to school, Adam. "Okay, so Adam brings up an important distinction between disability and impairment. He's right—the impairment in my legs still exists, regardless of elevators or ramps. They don't walk, won't walk, will never walk like yours do. And chronic pain makes this tricky, too, right? The limitations of pain aren't necessarily solved as easily as attaching a ramp to the side of a building, and, in a lot of tangible ways, the impairment it brings debilitates from the inside out. But for now, let's start with the simpler example of a paralyzed person getting to the third floor of a building. When I take an elevator up to our classroom, the need for walking has been eliminated. My paralysis isn't really a problem in this context. I'm not limited in any meaningful way as long as I have an accessible route to get here. In fact, right now in this room, we're all seated— there's no meaningful difference between my body and yours." The kids look even more confused than they did before. I'm starting to feel like I'm giving a lecture on how the royal family are immortal shape-shifting lizards. The uncertainty I feel from my students makes me question myself. Their resistance to these ideas is disorienting.

Because they're not comprehensively wrong. There *is* a layer of their narrative that makes sense. There are parts of my body that feel like a problem I'd like to fix. Even as I type this, I'm having a particularly high pain day, and my legs won't stop spasming—they jerk and tense, stiffen and shudder—and the computer resting on them keeps getting bumped around. If I'm being perfectly honest, living with this pain is infuriating. I've been working hard to find a way to manage these symptoms, and all of it—the pain, the spasms, the quest for relief—is exhausting. But this layer of truth isn't the one we're focusing on as a class, because it's the overwhelming default. It's so much easier to see the one disabled person and say, *She needs a cure so she can fit into our world!* It's much less common, much harder to recognize, *We need to change our world to fit more people.* And here's the key: When I trace the most painful threads in my story, when I gather the most defining memories of my life, these legs of mine are not The Most Debilitating Problem. At least, not in the way outsiders expect. When I look back and evaluate the most limiting, painful parts of my life, or even, more specifically, the hardest parts about being disabled, it's just not my legs. It's stigma, isolation, erasure, misunderstanding, skepticism, and ubiquitous inaccessibility. And that part—right there—is the social model understanding of what it's like to live in an ableist world when you're disabled. Despite all that, my paralyzed legs are the only thing outsiders seem to see.

"A person is either disabled or not," another floppy-haired boy says. His tone is sharper than mere confusion. He sounds irritated, maybe even combative, and his sentiment seems to resonate with others. My head is swirling with a hundred ideas and examples and scenarios and questions to push against this common oversimplification, and in an instant, they tangle.

I don't understand. If any demographic has the capacity to digest abstract theory and try on alternate ways of looking at the world, I expect it to be the ones sitting in this room. They're members of a generation so much more open to recognizing the unique position of any given identity, an age overwhelmed by unchecked idealism, a distinct group of youths known for their intellectual capacity. Am I an awful teacher? Or, just delusional? Has my personal connection to this material totally distorted my ability to think clearly about it? My mind is spinning, but there are twenty sets of eyes on me, all waiting for me to explain myself.

"Okay, let's try this," I say, trying to keep my voice chipper and casual. "Imagine a deaf woman who knows sign language walks into a room full of people signing. In this context, she has every ability to communicate with the group, ask questions, express her needs, make jokes. Now imagine that you enter that same room with your hearing ears. Does anyone in here know sign language?" They shake their heads, no. "So when you enter that space, *you* are the one who lacks access, can't communicate, is on the outside, right? The person sitting in the 'disabled' seat is flipped depending on the context. It just so happens that most spaces are designed for your access, but there are other ways this could go."

"But the woman in this scenario still can't hear," Adam insists. "I don't see how her lack of hearing could be considered anything other than a deficit, a biological defect." The thrust of his emphasis, the sourness of his tone, takes my breath away. I'm aware that Adam's is a common point of view he's inherited from those who put these ideas into motion well before he was born—a legacy none of us has fully escaped. I can almost feel Alexander Graham Bell in the room with us, proposing legislation that would keep "deaf-mute" people from marrying and reproducing in hopes that we could rid the human gene pool of these traits. But this might be the first time someone has argued this position to my face. It's definitely the first time it's been placed before me in a room full of teenagers as I sit with my "defected" body in front of my carefully crafted slides. Perhaps even more painful than the bite of his words is the silence from the rest of the group. I wait for anyone to challenge him or ask a follow-up question. They don't, and suddenly, I feel extraordinarily alone and dangerously vulnerable.

$$* \quad * \quad *$$

When I think back on this conversation now, the original loneliness doesn't sting so much. I mean, I was asking a group of very young people to rethink their basic understanding of the world. This was always going to be messy. Most of them had only ever considered disability as a catastrophic tragedy, an unfortunate error. Most of them had little capacity to fathom the gain that can accompany loss. Their response to concepts that remain unwieldy for many intelligent adults happened to bruise my forearms, but I'd invited them into that brawl without wearing any armor. I'd been living in an academic, disability bubble, and without realizing it, I'd volunteered to burst it in a high school among kids who had never had to confront these ideas. Some awful shit was bound to surface.

After that lecture, I went home deflated, embarrassed, and full of dread for the months ahead. With only a few hours left in the day before it was time to do it all again, I started frantically revising my lesson plan for the next day. If this were a movie, this would be the point where we transition into a heart-wrenching but ultimately uplifting montage. The music would build toward a victorious crescendo with clips capturing the leap from confusion to enlightenment, hostility to joy, frustration to smooth sailing. After beating her head against the wall trying to connect with this group of kids, the disabled teacher finds the key! She breaks down their barriers, one by one, and brings disability to life for this group of students. Finally, after buckets of sweat and tears, she watches as their eyes sparkle with hard-earned recognition. Yeah, turns out this wasn't a movie.

* * *

In real life, none of this process is cohesive or linear. Some students find sparkling moments of connection, then seem to lose interest. Some are always on top of their tasks, while others become increasingly agitated and restless. So I spend the rest of the semester throwing everything at the wall, hoping something will stick. I swivel from theoretical and abstract to pragmatic and cultural. I introduce the concept of disability as an identity, and to my horror, one trio of students essentially turns the conversation into a brainstorming session of all the reasons the world would be better if disability were entirely erased from the surface of the earth. I know this was a theoretical exercise for them. For me, I swear, it felt like eavesdropping on the future leaders of the world as they drew up a proposal for the elimination of my community.

I take what feels like a risk and invite them into my personal world for a day. Maybe I'm the barrier and hearing me tell my own stories will be the connection we need. I show them my Instagram account and take them through some of the pictures and stories I've posted there—pictures and stories intended to complicate traditional tropes and invite people into the most personal textures of a disabled life. This makes some of them more engaged and others even more defensive. We watch classic films, clips from Netflix, TED Talks. We spend time unpacking *Me Before You*, a 2016 film that earned an angry backlash from the disability community by reducing the experience of disability to one very privileged man's oversimplified desire to die in his quadriplegic body rather than be a burden to the women he loves. We read passionate, articulate critiques from disabled writers about the precise ways this movie harmed the disability community. In response, I read several student papers arguing that the disability community should stop complaining about skewed media portrayals—*they're just stories!* They research some of the starkest inequalities in the disability community. Some of them seem stirred by the profound injustices they find, while others seem too uncomfortable to look this in the face. We read a beautifully strange book called *Geek Love* about a very fictional family of circus freaks, and most of the reactions are bewilderment. (I mean, understood. It's a delightful book, but true-blue weird.) Mostly, I am flailing, and they seem just as lost.

During a discussion about a chapter from Andrew Solomon's book *Far from the Tree*, I invite them to explore the blurry relationship between illness and identity. Solomon grew up at a time when many people still considered being gay an illness. Later in adulthood, working as a psychologist and writer, he was amazed to find compelling overlaps between his experience as a gay man and the vibrant identity and pride he'd stumbled upon in the Deaf community. Originally, he'd seen deafness as nothing more than a defect. A loss. The more time he spent with those in the Deaf community, the more he listened to their stories, the more he recognized something familiar. Like most gay children born to straight parents, many deaf people are born to hearing parents. Like Solomon experienced in childhood with his own straight parents who longed for him to be straight, he learned that many deaf kids are encouraged, or even forced, to match the hearing world of their parents as much as possible. It's only later, often in adolescence, that they discover others like themselves and a sense of identity in the characteristic that makes them different. "I thought that if gayness, an identity, could grow out of homosexuality, an illness, and Deafness, an identity, could grow out of deafness, an illness, then there must be many other categories in this awkward interstitial territory," Solomon writes.

"This doesn't feel like a fair comparison," one of the quieter girls in the class says. She spends most days drawing elaborate doodles in the margins of her notebooks or staring out the window. I'm ecstatic to hear her voice in our conversation.

"There are definitely limits to this comparison," I say. "Being gay and being disabled are not the same thing. In fact, there are lots of ways that they're fundamentally different. But let's talk it through. What feels unfair about this comparison?" Her engagement with this idea feels fragile, and I try to tread delicately. I don't want to break the thread she's pulled.

"Well, there's no real reason a person wouldn't want to be gay. There's nothing wrong with it," she reasons.

"You're absolutely right—there is nothing wrong with being gay. But it's interesting your argument hinges on the assumption that there *is* something inherently wrong with being disabled." I pause. This is the idea so many of them can't loosen their grip on. I try another angle. "Right here and now, we can look at being gay and recognize that there is nothing wrong with it. But not so long ago, most people in our society were still sold on the idea that there was something biologically, socially, morally, and evolutionarily wrong with being gay. We built a hostile environment for gay people to live in, then used that harshness as evidence that being gay was an inferior path to follow. When Andrew Solomon's parents wished for him to be straight, part of this was a desire to protect him from a life that was surely going to be made more difficult, not because he was inherently defective, but because the world had been set up to punish him. I mean, you guys, being gay was considered an illness in the United States until *1973*. Can you believe that? A lot of your parents were born before then. Your grandparents were full-fledged adults living life surrounded by this way of thinking. Things have even changed in your short lifetimes—when you were born, it wasn't legal in all fifty states of this country to get married to someone of the same sex. That didn't happen until—what—three years ago? Today, most people in our country see that being gay is just another way of being in the world—another identity worth celebrating—but that wasn't always the case. And that's still not the case in a lot of places."

"Okay, yes, but all of that is just ignorance," she interjects. "Bigoted people making life harder for gay people. There's still nothing *inherently* wrong with being gay. Like, a gay person isn't *defective*. They're literally just attracted to the same sex. Being disabled is just something in your body not working right."

Here we are again, right where we started. My whole body
sighs before continuing. It was easy for them to see the value in
gay culture, gay identity, gay pride. I wondered why it was so difficult to see even a shred of value in disability. "That's the crux of
it, isn't it? Is it possible for disability to be anything other than a
defect? If identities are built around defining characteristics, can
disability represent another form of difference worthy of community, celebration, identification?"

As my students start packing up their backpacks, I talk faster.
"At the very least, it's worth thinking about the possibility of
disability as a *neutral* category, an experience with highs and
lows not unlike those of nondisabled folks. . . ." They break eye
contact, already mentally in their next class, running through
questions for their upcoming physics quiz. "And on that note,
we'll pick up this discussion tomorrow!" I call after them as they
head to their next classes.

When I think back on this conversation, I wish I had simply
said: *A group is marginalized because society marginalizes them.
Society also has the power to change that. What would it mean for
disabled folks if society saw us as acceptable, equal, valuable parts
of the whole?* Although, it's an impossible game, I'm trying to
find the perfect combinations of words to unlock the code. I'm
not sure there were any magic phrases that could break all the
way through the intricate and constantly reinforced narrative
of ableism. That takes time, experience, and a desire to understand, I've learned. As the semester continues, it often feels
like students are simply becoming more entrenched in their
original ideologies. Disability can be *only* a loss, a defect, a de-

ficiency, a problem to solve or eliminate. I don't know how to pull out of this cycle.

But there are moments over the course of the semester that feel victorious. The smallest signs of understanding set off heavenly bells that can ring for days: The afternoon I describe the Capitol Crawl protests in 1990 that led to passage of the Americans with Disabilities Act, and they all wonder why not one of them has ever heard this part of US history. The student who researches the history of institutionalization and concludes her presentation with a stunning, insightful description of the larger patterns of exclusion and erasure surrounding the disability community. The day we Skype with writer, pole dancer, wheelchair-user, and self-proclaimed "International Sex Icon" Erin Clark, and one student asks, "Do you wish there was a cure for your disability?" Erin answers honestly, with raw reflection, self-aware contradiction, and rich complexity, and my students get to witness her waltz gracefully through this gray area without the easy answer so many of them expected.

Around mid-semester, star-of-the-soccer-team Adam arrives in my office. "I've been trying to have an open mind about this class," he starts, "but I just can't bring myself to care about anything we're reading or talking about. I mean, none of this has anything to do with me or will ever matter to me."

I don't know what expression I make with my face or how much time goes by before I speak. I'm not surprised he feels this way. He's already made his position pretty clear in every conversation and assignment. But I'm stunned that he feels no shame saying it out loud. To my face. When I'd started teaching this class months before, I'd been fully convinced that I was about to teach these kids some of the most exciting, valuable, universally relevant, revolutionary ideas they'd ever come across. I could see a new future just over the horizon, and we were going to build it together with education, collaboration, imagination, and care.

Has it been two seconds of silence? Twenty minutes? I'm not sure. "Well, Adam," I finally say. "The fact that you have a body means that this class is relevant to you."

"Yeah . . . but I don't have a *disabled* body." He talks slowly, methodically. He seems confused that I've missed this most obvious detail.

"You have a body that meets some form of access or limitation at every turn," I insist. I can see this from where I sit. While I'm less sure what his limitations are, I can see the buildings and trails, the career paths and media representations that have all been built with him in mind. "That doesn't interest you?"

"No, not really," he trails off.

He seems as baffled by me as I am by him. He continues to resist, I continue to counter, and our conversation goes nowhere. I take another approach. "Okay, let me ask you this." If he really can't find any way to connect with this content, maybe we can think about this from the opposite angle—maybe he can find the curiosity to understand a group whose lives are considerably different from his own. Maybe the goal should be to provide a setting where he can practice caring about people he perceives as categorically, comprehensively different from himself. "If we were reading stories about the experiences of Indigenous people in this country, would you feel more invested?"

"No, not really," he says. Wow, this kid has no shame.

"The experiences of women?" I ask.

"Well, yeah. I'd care about that."

"Why?"

"Women are a part of my life," he says.

Okay, is this kid messing with me now? Or is he doing these gymnastics in his own brain? He's working so hard to pretend that disabled people aren't a part of his world—could never be a part of his world—when he literally has a disabled woman for a teacher making direct eye contact with him at this very moment. I've never seen anyone work so hard to not care.

That whole semester, I feel like I'm trying to drive my car up a mudslide. No matter how hard I pump the gas, rotate my steering wheel, or put the car in reverse, my tires just keep spinning, sinking deeper and deeper into the sloppy mud.

There are some moments—exchanges, expressions, and student papers—that bolster me. I try to focus on the one kid making eye contact during a lecture, or the tiny signs of understanding in the third paragraph of that one paper. One afternoon, Sophia stays after class. She's one of those kids who's always smiling and nodding at me during a lecture, even on the days when almost all of her peers are on their phones or doing homework for other classes. Today, as she slowly packs her notebook and pens into her backpack, she's telling me how devastated she was by a scene in Susan Nussbaum's *Good Kings, Bad Kings*. (No spoilers, but it's about a group of disabled juveniles living in an institution together, and it does not shy away from some of the harshest realities of being poor and disabled.) Sophia's not the first person to express distress about this particular scene, but her distress seems to live in a slightly different location. Unlike a lot of kids who came into our classroom shocked that they'd been subjected to a book with such horrifying content, Sophia seems upset that the scene represents the experiences of living human beings in our world. I express as much to her. I'm trying to emphasize the beauty in her empathy, but I'm pretty sure some of my weariness in the class's general apathy seeps out.

Sophia pauses. It looks like she's sorting out what to say back, and I'm immediately uncomfortable. I don't want her taking on my feelings about the overwhelming weight of indifference in our classroom, so I start rambling about the book, and Sophia interrupts me.

"Dr. Taussig," she says, looking me straight in the eye. "I love this school and the people in it, but our worlds can be very small. We need conversations like this."

Her acknowledgment takes my breath away. She doesn't say that every concept we've discussed in class makes perfect, immediate sense, and I know at least part of this course has felt uncomfortable to her. Instead, she insists that understanding the experience of disability is worth our time and energy—a sentiment worlds away from Adam's determined disinterest.

Even with glimmers and sparks from curious students who do want to explore and understand—even with Sophia's powerful acknowledgment—going to class each day starts to feel like jumping into an ice-cold pool. My body stiffens before each conversation. I hold my breath, just trying to survive. Five days a week, eight hours a day. There is no distance, no buffer, no relief from these exchanges.

After a particularly brutal discussion with one of my classes, I go to an antique shop with Micah. We've been there countless times, and it's usually a happy escape. This day, the entire space feels altered, like I've swallowed a pill that throws an eerie wash over everything around me. As I push myself through the cluttered rows of old books and funky lamps, around groups of friends trying on hats and clusters of women peering at price tags through bifocals, I feel my students' comments pulsing through the crowds: *Disability is nothing but a defect. The world would be better if disability were removed from it.* While I might have wondered before, I feel certain now: this is what everyone is thinking, what everyone has always been thinking. The past few years I'd been living in an academic bubble, but my students had confirmed what I'd always known in my gut. They'd lifted the curtain and revealed a world that wanted no part of me. I feel anxious and shaky, unwanted and in the way. I can't warm the chill that has crept into my shoulders. I want to hide. Stop trying. Bury myself in blankets and a steady stream of *The Great British Bake Off*.

✳ ✳ ✳

That semester, the voices of skepticism in the room swallowed me whole, but distance also allows me to recognize all the students, like Sophia, who were willing to imagine and explore this space with me. While I struggled to keep them in my line of vision at the time, I now hold on to my memory of those kids with gratitude and hope. It's almost embarrassing to remember the squishy ease with which I lost myself teaching this class. How little pushback I could withstand before I doubted my thirty years of firsthand experience, my PhD in disability studies. I had leaped into this with the greatest naivete, with no preparation for the pain of teaching material with such high personal stakes to a group of teenagers, most of whom hadn't thought more than thirty seconds about disability in their seventeen years on earth; all of whom were consumed by college applications, a bunch of other classes, and a host of extracurricular activities; none of whom had electively signed up to take this class.

Now, it's so much easier to see: When I first introduced my students to the social and medical models of disability on that afternoon early in the fall semester, I wasn't teaching them something I just pulled from the standard curriculum. When I brought them disabled characters and writers to analyze, I wasn't cobbling together ideas found on an English teaching blog. Like a kid bringing a handful of precious roly-polies she'd found buried in the damp beneath the heaviest rock in the yard, hands open cradling her delicate treasure, I was sharing with them some of the most personal, most earth-shifting ideas I'd gathered from my time in graduate school, from the entirety of my life. I hadn't realized the tenderness swathed around my academic training, and they, of course, had no way of comprehending these fragile layers.

Back when I was nearly a year into my PhD program and

moments away from quitting the whole damn thing, I read
my first bit of disability studies. I was sitting in my ugly green
velvet chair, weary with academic-speak, disillusioned by how
little any of this seemed to matter, entirely uninterested in the
stiff and stifled ideas I was sacrificing sleep, financial stability,
and my well-being to study, when I opened an email from a
friend who'd sent me an attachment he thought I might be
interested in reading—Lennard Davis's introduction "Disability, the Missing Term in the Race, Class, Gender Triad" (from
his book *Enforcing Normalcy: Disability, Deafness and the Body*).
On the surface, this title sang the same pompous tune of the
twenty other articles I'd read that month. (Why so many lists
of three and colons, academia?) At the same time, even just
seeing the word "disability" printed in an academic title with
such authority stirred me. It was published when I was nine
years old, and here I was, nearly twenty years later, download-
ing it onto my laptop.

"Disability," I read, "is not an object—a woman with a cane—
but a social process that intimately involves everyone who has a
body and lives in the world of the senses." I was stunned. What
was he saying? It was as if I'd spent years acting my part in an
elaborate stage performance, squinting under a relentless spotlight I hadn't even known was there, baking under the heat of
one steady lamp, unable to see past the edge of my paralyzed
legs. Wasn't this just life? Suddenly, the spotlight moved to my
left and I could see the set behind me, the chairs in front of
me. What was this feeling? This relief? Disability isn't just *me*?
Located in my scrawny legs that drag instead of lift? Carried in

the scars running down the length of my spine and the edges of
my hip bones? Disability is something that expands beyond me?
That involves everyone? This was my first experience hearing
someone describe the forces that had remained entirely invisible
and wildly powerful throughout my life. I'd always sensed people in an audience, other actors on the stage, and an elaborate
set, but no one else confirmed they existed, so I'd tried to ignore
them.

I lapped up his words as he continued, "the object of disability
studies is not the person using the wheelchair or the Deaf person but the set of social, historical, economic, and cultural pro-
cesses that regulate and control the way we think about and think
through the body." The words sent tingles down my face, shoulders, arms, and through my pores. They caught me in the back of
the throat and sprouted through my tear ducts. What if I wasn't
just a broken version of a whole person? What if I wasn't "the
problem," the burden, the thing to fix? I could feel the physics of
the universe shifting around me. This was my very own *Truman
Show* moment, only the big reveal brought with it relief and
power.

My brain was sparking, my heart was thumping, I couldn't
slow down, I just kept devouring the words until I ran straight
into a story that made me stop. Davis explained that the "impulse" to gawk at, push aside, erase, or eradicate the disabled
body is not an inherent human trait. This is not some deep-
seated "survival of the fittest" drive designed to keep us alive.
Instead, he argues that this reaction to disability is learned. To
illustrate, he tells a story:

One student told me that her mother had no fingers on one hand. As a child she had never considered this particularly strange, and she was always surprised when strangers stared at her mother's hand. To her it was a loving, caressing hand that she might joke about, kiss, or hold. The point is not that she was habituated to what others might consider a horror, but that she had not received the instruction to cast the hand away.

The image felt like a thwap to my gut. I recognized the intimacy between the child and her mother's hand. I felt it in my own bones. The familiarity released a valve holding back my tears, and once it was turned, I couldn't shut it off. This comfort, this affection, this safety between the disabled body and the ones who love it was a feeling I'd felt before, a long time ago. This was me with my family, with my siblings, scrambling around like puppies in a box. In our backyard on my hands and knees, dragging myself up to the top bunk, sitting with my legs bent in unexpected directions—to the siblings who grew up with me, I was always, simply Rebekah: their little sister who talked like a baby much too long, hogged the sugar bowl at breakfast, and scabbed up her knees crawling around the neighborhood. The memory of this easy, comprehensive acceptance crushed me. It still does—to close my eyes, feel its gift, and know there's no real way to get back to that exact place.

That night, Lennard Davis took me through my introduction to the social model of disability, point by point. In a process that felt like actual sparks of magic, his words became a tool I could

use to dismantle some of the sturdiest narratives that had dic-
tated my self-perception, my life choices, my interactions with
the people around me. These were stories that had been reinforced over a lifetime, stories that had ingrained in me the very
mindset my students found themselves nodding so comfortably
along with, the perspectives that had done tremendous work to
silently, steadily place the labels of Defect, Burden, Outsider,
and Problem around my neck. The medical model had taught
me early and consistently that my body—my presence in any
given space—was an object to puzzle over, poke for study, push
to the fringes, and try to fix.

The medical and social models of disability aren't theoretical to
me. They are just as much a part of my days as gravity or Netflix.
They are always, always there. I'd expected my students to feel
this with me, to access these theories the way I had, to experience them with the same sensations. Of course, this was never
going to happen. Could never happen. And if I'd known my
expectations, I could have prepared myself for this. But I hadn't
realized just how tangled up my most vulnerable life stories were
with these theoretical models until I tried to teach them. As I
sat in front of those kids, pointing to slides with bullet-point
definitions, I was also carrying personal scars inflicted by the
medical model over a lifetime. They saw a definition to write
down in their notebooks, but for me, the medical model wasn't
just a theoretical ideology. I'd absorbed it into my own body. I'd
believed it more than anyone.

I wasn't sure whether I could bear to teach a class on disability studies ever again. My first semester proved just how difficult

it could be to recognize and value an understanding of these two lenses, let alone practice looking through them. Although I still believed that grappling with these ideas in a classroom was vital work, I wasn't sure I had the fortitude for a second round.

＊ ＊ ＊

On the last day of class, I mention that this might be the last semester I work through this material with students, and some of them seem surprised, which takes me off guard. It's my first clue that they really don't understand what this class has been like for me. It highlights how differently we experienced these months together. As much as they'll never be able to grasp what it felt like for me to sit through our conversations, I'm certain I'll never know what they took from the class. I often find myself wondering, though: Will any of our discussions or readings come back to them as they get older, experience more, interact with more people, get some distance from childhood, have their own children? Will they surprise themselves by the perspectives they're able to offer in conversations about representation or healthcare? Will they even remember where these ideas first sprouted?

One of the other English teachers I work with says that teachers' fists are full of seeds, and we spend our days throwing them across the concrete pavement, never knowing when or where one of those seeds will take root or what plant might start pushing its way through the cracks. I haven't decided whether I find this picture comforting or not.

I do know that being the only visibly disabled body in a room of seventeen- and eighteen-year-olds while trying to persuade them to care about school, let alone about the real experiences and representations of disabled people—to challenge all they think they understand about bodies and norms and identity—is a recipe for discomfort. For all of us. I've learned that the dismantling of ableism can be a violent process, and bearing witness from your front row seat probably means you'll end up catching some of the blows. I saw my own idealism drain in this space and felt the loss. I also know that discomfort can be a sign of growth. And I think growth is worth discomfort. (Usually? To a certain extent?) At the end of the day, despite the darkness and loss, the strain and bruises, I do see that I grew, and I don't think I was the only one.

So, like a genuinely reckless person who can't have lost every shred of her idealism, I decide to give the class another go. This time, though, I make some fundamental adjustments. I intentionally provide more possible points of connection for the kids. I take care to protect myself a bit more. Instead of focusing exclusively on the disabled body, I expand the curriculum to look at the narrow scripts we've written for other bodies, too, like gender-nonconforming bodies and fat bodies. I use the medical and social models of disability as tools to investigate a broader set of questions exploring the notion of "cures" and "fixes." I ask questions like: How much of the human body do we want to cure? What should be fixed and what should be left alone? What is the purpose of categorizing bodies, and what do we lose when we do it? What do we

lose when we fixate on a cure? Is physical health more important than well-being, mental health, or pride in one's identity?
What is normal, and is it an ideal goal?

On the first day of class, I ask the group whether they have
any idea what this course is going to be about. No one does. *Here
we go!* I prepare myself for another semester with uninterested,
unengaged students.

During the first weeks of the semester, I assign them a
series of articles from the disability section of the *New York
Times* written by a few disabled writers thinking through what
"cure" means to them. At first, our conversations sound like
a taped recording of the previous semester: *It's foolish to push
against a cure that would make life so much better for everybody.
Disabled people shouldn't feel threatened by a push for a cure—they
don't have to get it if they don't want it, so why do they care?*

Then, without any prompting and seemingly out of nowhere,
one of my students brings the conversation to a very personal
place. He tells the story of getting diagnosed with attention
deficit/hyperactivity disorder (ADHD). He talks about medication and identity. He describes what it feels like to be in his
brain from hour to hour, the unique challenges it brings, but also
the joy and abundance. His story adds life to our discussion. It
also sparks more stories.

Apparently, we quickly learn, four other students in our class
of fourteen are diagnosed with ADHD. They all start telling
their own stories, how it felt to be diagnosed, and what it feels
like to be in their bodies. Some of them express a sense of pride

and identity in having ADHD, while others say it is entirely insignificant to their sense of self. Some say they'd never take medication for it, while others say medication has changed their lives. Our conversation runs over into the next class, and we have to pull ourselves away from it. Not everyone participates, but for most of the group, we discover so much more to ask and share. This becomes a class pattern. We always run out of time to explore.

The last weeks of the semester are my favorite, because I send students out on their own to investigate the ideas discovered in our class. "It's your turn to interrogate this impulse we have to pathologize and fix some bodies and accommodate others. Where else do you see this happening? What patterns do you see unfolding around you?" They come back with so much—more bodies, more connections, more questions. They ask: *How does rhetoric dictate the way we look at fatness? What drives us to pursue cosmetic surgery, and is this a bad thing? Is makeup a medium for empowerment? Does the cosmetics industry reinforce beliefs in our bodies' insufficiencies? How do we navigate the burgeoning field of gene therapy and "designer babies"? Who gets to decide what traits are worth propagating? And how?*

I don't know how to measure what this group will take with them from our time together. I have no clue whether they'll remember the medical and social models of disability when they set off to their college campuses next year, whether any of these ideas will come back to them when they vote in their first elections, or get their first jobs. I do know that we explored a whole lot of shit together. That we went on a roller coaster ride of rethinking some of the most deeply ingrained beliefs we carry as a culture. And this is not small.

* * *

I'm not teaching this class again for a while. I'm ready for some distance, ready to try something new. But a couple of weeks ago with my ninth-grade English class, we were working through a book when I started to notice that the social and medical models of disability felt relevant to the story, so I decided to give the lenses to that group of fourteen-year-olds. Because who knows what plant might start to push its way through the cracks? I adapted my slides to be a bit more ninth-grade friendly, I told more stories, I used the same image of the woman at the bottom of the stairs, and I didn't expect the information to transform their souls or worlds. They listened attentively, they did their best to apply it to the book we were reading, and most of them didn't seem to grasp the big picture.

And then. Three days later, Claire calls out to me while the class is getting settled. Claire is a ball of nerves. She's usually trying to sneak her phone out during class and can't stop chatting to whatever human person she's sitting next to, especially when I'm giving instructions. In other words, she doesn't stand out as a kid I'd expect to remember all that much from her English class.

Today she says, "Dr. Taussig! I saw this ad that reminded me of what you were talking to us about the other day."

"Oh, yeah?" I say, trying my best to listen to her while I take attendance. "What ad?"

"It was for this adaptive controller thing?" she says. "It didn't have so many buttons, and it had this smooth surface, and they had all these kids with disabilities that were playing video games with it, and it was just like we were talking about."

Suddenly, I forget about attendance. "The Xbox adaptive controller?" I ask. Poor Claire has just become my reason for teaching, my life's fulfillment, my favorite thing.

"Yeah, yeah!" she says.

"Claire! That's a perfect example of what we were talking about!" I feel like hugging her, and I might cry right there. "I mean, instead of just assuming video games aren't for disabled folks, they played with the setup to invite more players to the game! And the adaptive controller makes playing video games so much more accessible for so many more people, right? Old people or people who are less coordinated or someone just learning to play the game!"

"Yeah. It just reminded me of what you were talking about," she says, not quite matching my wild-eyed intensity, maybe a tad bewildered by my overwhelming, face-splitting enthusiasm, but I feel fine with that, because I see the smallest bit of green pushing through the concrete.

4

THE REAL CITIZENS OF LIFE

I don't think I was the only middle-school girl obsessed with imagining my life as an adult. *What will I look like? Where will I live? How many bridesmaids will I have, and what will my wedding dress look like?* Living in a pre-Pinterest world, I cut out pictures from magazines that helped me imagine my beautiful future life—pictures of happy brides and sophisticated women with shimmering hair and smoldering men with well-fitted suits—and taped them onto my closet door, tucked them into the frame of my dresser mirror, and glued them to poster board that I labeled with silvery gel pens.

One elaborate fantasy sequence is recorded in my Anne Geddes diary. Here are the basic details of my thirteen-year-old dream world: I have long shiny hair. I live by myself in an apartment with every hair and makeup product I've ever wanted, including spray lotion and yummy-smelling shampoo that costs lots of money. I have a wardrobe of classy pencil skirts and silky blouses for my job. I work in some office overlooking a nondescript city doing something creative that keeps me very busy in a fulfilling sort of way. I have a boyfriend named Nathan who calls me to see whether I can get away from the office for a quick lunch, but I'm just too busy with a series of vague projects, so instead he offers to take me to dinner (the fancy kind, of course). I'm late to dinner, because I'm just so busy and important, but Nathan waits anyway, because he just loves me so much. We have an imprecise kind of fun at dinner, and then Nathan drops me off at home with a Bath & Body Works bag of products that I go use—alone?

In every scene, there is one doozy of a detail: my body has no trace of disability. Through all of this, Adult Rebekah walks gracefully down the street and up the stairs to her chic apartment.

Perhaps most striking to me about this fantasy is that it never ever struck me as silly or unrealistic to erase the fundamental mechanics of the body in which I lived. At thirteen, I was already permanently disabled, and yet I felt compelled to leap over this unchanging fact so I could dream up a life of fulfilling work and male adoration. *Why?*

Without having the words at the time, this was the universe as I had come to understand it: On the one hand, there were the Real Citizens of Life—the ones this whole planet was built for, who were beautiful and capable and desired. They were the ones who fell in love and had careers and families and dramas at school and stories worth knowing. They were worthy of jealousy, love songs, and starring roles. I knew who they were, because their images flooded every screen, every magazine page, every billboard, every CD cover. They populated the sitcoms, movies, and music videos. They were the cast of *Saved by the Bell*, *Friends*, and *Dawson's Creek*. They were the Spice Girls and the Backstreet Boys. They were Jack and Rose, Allie and Noah. And then there was me.

I internalized my role early and continued to be reminded of it with consistent reinforcement. With experience and time, I learned that the best I had to offer society was to inspire the Real Citizens of Life by smiling on the sidelines, being joyful despite my wheelchair. I was a tool for keeping them grateful and motivated to seize their days. I was here to teach them the loftier nuggets of wisdom, like how to live life to the fullest—to provide an opportunity to prove that they were really a good character. I wasn't here to fall in love, become a parent, broker the deal, crack the case, offer sex appeal, save the damsel, or be president. If I forgot my part—even for a moment—or attempted to audition for another position in the story, there was always another character there to nudge me back to that little piece of tape on the stage marking my spot.

As I've gotten older, I can see it even more clearly—the elaborate stage performance with assigned roles that we, as a culture, perform together. For most of us, we learn how to play our parts as we go along. We pay attention to cues, we watch how the other characters interact with us, we see what happens when we step outside of our designated roles, and soon, we learn the precise parameters of the characters we play in this story. Some of us get parts as the Real Citizens of Life, and we strive very hard to hold on to these sparkly roles, terrified of losing our positions, or anxious we're about to be discovered as frauds. Or some of us hardly realize the role has been handed to us at all. What other part would we play? Most are denied these prominent roles and are sent immediately to the margins.

For a good while I really did think I was the only one on the outside. It took some time to realize that others—many others—were there with me. For those of us playing secondary characters, we learn to fit in tiny boxes where we try our best to live without letting our arms dangle too far over the sides.

When I was about seventeen years old with a freshly laminated driver's license and a new (to me) 1993 white Buick Century spruced up with simple hand controls, I drove myself to the bookstore. With practiced ease I swung my wheelchair out of the car, attached the wheels, bounced into it, and felt capable and breezy as I pushed myself across the parking lot toward the front doors. When I arrived, a man and woman were already opening the first set of doors to the shop. I thanked them as I moved toward the second set of doors, naturally arriving first. Happily, I opened the second set of doors for them, reciprocating the courtesy I had just been given. As the couple walked through, I heard the woman mutter, not too quietly, "She's a proud little thing, isn't she." I felt the sting and heard myself laugh with surprise. *What was that?* Even before I had the words, I knew: I had stepped out of line. Silly me! I'd been operating under the belief that I could be the newly independent leading lady, brightly bounding through her story, but I'd already been assigned my role as the Weak Girl, here to affirm to the Real Citizens of Life that they were a thoughtful pair offering a friendly hand.

In my late twenties, I moved into a little house with two cranky cats, and Micah moved in shortly after. Maybe a year later, after seeing us do life together month after month, my neighbor stopped us on our way out to the movies. "So, I have to ask. Are you two brother and sister?" He seemed genuinely puzzled, which I suppose makes sense, considering he'd seen us holding hands, kissing, and flirting for the previous twelve months. As I'd been busy living out my life as the star of my own romance story, he'd been busy trying to figure out what narrative made more sense: the Helpless Asexual Girl with a boyfriend, or two siblings in love. How far must he stretch his imagination to see me and my chair as a legitimate romantic interest? It seems it was hardly fathomable to him. I took a beat, tilted my head, and looked back at him. "No," I said, amused and not laughing. "He's not my brother."

During the last year of graduate school, I traveled a lot. Near the end of a road trip culminating in a visit to Albuquerque where I presented my work at a professional conference, I'd driven 2,681 miles across the country. I'd rented cars (always taking the three extra steps required to book one with hand controls), booked hotels, put gas in my vehicles with my own money, and presented my original work to people who cared to listen. (To be perfectly honest, the room wasn't packed, but you better believe I gave the most animated talk.) I'd found my way around unfamiliar cities and felt my abilities stretch and hold me. As I was filling up a soda on my last stop, on my very last leg of my trip, I was feeling grounded and unstoppable—the star of a story about hard-earned professional fulfillment and personal peace on a solo road trip across the United States. This is also the precise moment a man I didn't know pushed a wad of ones and fives into my lap. "I was in a wheelchair for two years," he said. "I know what it's like." I looked at his bills, bewildered. Suddenly I was the Begging Cripple of this story, useless and desperate. "No. No, I don't feel comfortable," I said, pushing the money away. He kept talking, explaining just how much he understood, how he wanted to help people like me. His confidence in the story he was telling was louder than any other noise in the building. He was intimately familiar with the Begging Cripple role and stood tall in his part as the Compassionate Helper. Meanwhile, my brain turned into a flat white screen, searing and blank. I got back in my car, feeling so small.

It is a fact that a person with a disability is significantly less likely to be gainfully employed. This represents the lived experience of millions of people. But there are other ways to tell this story, other possible turns this script could take, other scenes waiting to be written. As much as I felt strong and unstoppable on that road trip, I felt just as deflated by the never-ending brawl required to maintain a sense of dignity belonging to a group that is perpetually framed as helpless.

Here's a question: What's more exhausting—being disabled or trying to shake off the roles that other people constantly expect you to fill? (I'm too tired to answer.)

Disabled people have been assigned a clear part in the stage performance. We are the recipients of help, in need of assistance, holding out a tin can for charity, here to inspire. Attempting to claim another role, a more complicated part, like the one who accepts *and* offers a bit of help, one who uses a chair to navigate the world *and* has sex, one who can't walk *and* isn't asking for your money—even if it's a role that feels natural and fitting—can surprise, confuse, or even irritate the other people in the performance.

When you live inside of the story, it can be difficult to see this dynamic. We begin to believe things like "this is just how it is—this is how the world works, like hydrogen bonds or gravity," forgetting that, while the very first authors of ableism may be long gone (whoever they were), we are still performing these outdated roles and—guess what?!—stories can change.

One of the spaces where we already and actively workshop these narratives is in the stories we tell on screens, through speakers, and on pages. We're currently in a time of great revision. We're opening our eyes to the limited scope of our previous stories and realizing there are way more voices to amplify in our narratives. Things have changed a lot since I was thirteen. It used to be assumed that movies, television, stand-up comedy, and advertising would feature a narrow, celebrated swath of our population, but there's been a slow shift away from that in the past decade or so. The Clint Eastwoods, Tom Cruises, and Matt Damons are no longer the only ones occupying our screens. Films like *Black Panther*, *Get Out*, *BlacKkKlansman*, and *Crazy Rich Asians* show that people are excited about good stories told with casts made up of nonwhite folks—and the box office sales and award show wins cosign this shift. While there is plenty of pushback—like men furious at the all-women cast of the 2016 version of *Ghostbusters* for so violently ripping apart their nostalgic memories from their mini-misogynistic childhoods—films like *Ocean's 8* and *Captain Marvel* demonstrate a continued investment to disrupt some of the most male-dominated franchises.

At the very least, the capitalist wheels of society have recognized that diversity sells. More people are gravitating toward inclusion, and where the people flock, so flocketh the money. Millennials and Gen Zers have proved that they are more likely to choose a brand that demonstrates a commitment to inclusivity, and so, in a matter of years, we've seen countless brands move in that direction. From Nike to Nine West, Snickers to Crocs, Tylenol to Sephora, more and more companies are choosing to feature the bodies and storylines of people of all sizes, shapes, backgrounds, abilities, gender expressions, skin pigmentations, sexualities, and ethnicities. For some advertising campaigns, like Billie razors and Aerie underwear, this includes so-called body flaws, like stretch marks and body hair. More companies are committing to minimizing or doing away with photoshopping models in their ads, including Dove and CVS. And this inclusivity isn't always limited to glossy ad pages. Target launched lines of adaptive clothing and "sensory-friendly" home items, including products like weighted blankets and cocoon seats for kids with a range of sensory needs. Microsoft came out with an adaptable Xbox controller that doesn't demand the same fine-motor precision of previous controllers.

So, wow, right? Look at all that big, bright, gorgeous, messy, real representation of humanity! Inclusivity is where it's at, the wave of the future, the place to be. But instead of checking the box on diversity (done!), this hard-earned progress only leads to more questions and considerations.

Mindy Kaling's film *Late Night* gives a brilliant snapshot of disability and storytelling today. It has the gloss and beat of a romantic comedy, but it tells the story of two women in the first and final acts of their careers, ultimately working to make the entertainment industry more inclusive. Kaling's character, Molly Patel, is a South Asian–American woman who finds herself working with a team of all-white, all-male writers on a late-night show hosted by Emma Thompson's character, Katherine Newbury. Molly shows up in the writing room with a fresh diagnosis for the show's growing staleness over the previous decade. She offers new jokes. She calls Katherine to a brave authenticity other writers aimed to erase. What a beautiful illustration of the ways inclusivity makes us richer, smarter, fuller, better. I'm here for this.

At the film's end, the camera pans across the new writers' room that Molly and Katherine assemble. In stark contrast to the film's early scenes, only like three white dudes are left at the table. The new working space is bursting with vibrant diversity.

Also: I didn't see a single disabled body at that table. What a stark reminder that even those most dedicated to inclusion rarely imagine disabled people into the scene.

Of course, disability is often invisible—present without an obvious signal or quick recognition. Many people with disabilities "pass" as nondisabled. In other words, it's possible that disability is still part of the imagined inclusive space in the final scene of *Late Night*. But I don't think it was on the radar for any of the writers, directors, producers, or performers of the film, because (1) the scene *is* full of people who are visibly pushing against the white/male status quo, and (2) the story *does* include one disabled character who plays a very different role in the story—Katherine's supportive, behind-the-scenes, heart-breakingly sick husband Walter (played by John Lithgow). Walter is a quiet and steady support to his wife (yay!), plays piano alone in the back room during his wife's glamorous party, and is quite unhappy about the deteriorating state of his body as he ages with Parkinson's disease. He's sweet and sad with a splash of victim.

There's nothing inherently awful about including this kind of character in a story about two strong women. This film isn't about husbands, and it's not about disability, and that's okay. But Walter's character and the final scene of the film reveal a whole staff of story-makers who agree that this, right here, is what vibrant, exciting, worthwhile inclusion looks like, and that, over there, is what disability looks like. The two are kept separate, a reality that reveals a team of skilled, educated, informed story-makers entirely unaware of disability as an identity that has something valuable to contribute—an identity worth explicitly inviting to the table.

It might slip under the radar or exist on the edges, but disability is actually *ev-er-y-where* in the stories around us. It's often used as a metaphor (Mr. Potter in *It's a Wonderful Life*, Colin in *The Secret Garden*), as a plot device (Raymond in *Rain*

Man, Melvin Udall in *As Good as It Gets*), or as a tool to inspire compassion, pity, or "softness" in nondisabled characters and audiences (Tiny Tim in *A Christmas Carol*, Joseph Merrick in *The Elephant Man*). Characters with impairments are depicted as either "super-crips" triumphing over life's adversities (Pollyanna and Forrest Gump) or pitiable, isolated victims who'd rather die than live in their impaired bodies (Maggie in *Million Dollar Baby*, Will in *Me Before You*). Oh, and sometimes we get to be villains (Captain Ahab, Captain Hook, Darth Vader) or thrown in the mix as objects to horrify (Doctor Poison in *Wonder Woman*, Ruben in *Midsommar*).

This is not to dismiss the strides that have been made in mainstream representation; shows like *Switched at Birth* and *Speechless* do more to normalize the respective experiences of deafness and cerebral palsy than ostracize them, and characters on shows like *CSI*, *Private Practice*, and *Stranger Things* happen to have impairments (shared by the actors performing the roles) that play little part in their active contribution to the plotlines. In 2019, Netflix came out with a genuinely funny, charming miniseries, *Special*, about a gay man with cerebral palsy that is written and performed by the real-life protagonist of the story, Ryan O'Connell. Marvel just announced that one of its upcoming films, *The Eternals*, will include a deaf superhero played by the deaf actress Lauren Ridloff. These examples are worthy of celebration but still remain the exception. More often than not, the stories we tell about disability are sappy or eerie or melodramatic or frightening distortions of actual experience.

It's more pleasant to pretend this is a problem of the past, especially when looking at clearly condescending or offensive portraits from earlier eras. But the skewed depictions of disability have only slipped into a twenty-first-century packaging that's harder to see through.

Let's take a closer look at one of the most lucrative international box office hits in history. In James Cameron's 2009 Academy Award–winning film *Avatar*, our hero, Jake Sully, is paralyzed during active duty with the Marines and is consumed with longing for freedom from his confinement. This reinforces the ableist belief that one surely cannot live a fulfilling life in a disabled body, especially when Jake's character finds power and contentment only when he enters an alternate world that restores his abilities.

To make this conversation even trickier, films doing powerful good for one group of people can simultaneously participate in reinforcing reductive stereotypes for another, as we see in Jordan Peele's thoughtful, smart, and rightfully celebrated *Get Out*. Even as the film gives a searing portrayal of liberal racism in twenty-first-century America, it leans on a tired disability trope—the chilling blind villain who will commit atrocious acts just for the chance to see again. It strikes me as a shorthand prop—like a screaming tea kettle or a cloaked figure hiding in the shadows coming into focus—to get the viewer to feel something, only this trope uses a marginalized group of people for an effect.

And this technique doesn't seem to be losing popularity. Even *Pokémon Detective Pikachu* peddles this same narrative to children; the supervillain plaguing the city is an angry Bill Nighy in a wheelchair who recklessly manipulates and destroys, driven by a violent passion to restore his body to its original abilities. Poor Micah regretted sitting next to me in the movie theater as I whisper-yelled at the screen, "Learn how to tell a new story, you ableist toad pots! You're a hundred years late! This is *boring*!"

Another common trope affirms that disabled characters are always longing for a "whole" body through a fantasy sequence—a moment of respite from the burden of disability to relish a "pure," working body, even just for an imaginary moment. Fox's celebrated *Glee* includes the scene where Artie (Kevin McHale) jumps out of his wheelchair for a full dance sequence; James Marsh's 2014 Academy Award–winning film *The Theory of Everything* shows Stephen Hawking (Eddie Redmayne) getting out of his wheelchair to walk across the floor and pick up a woman's fallen pen; Guillermo del Toro's gorgeous 2017 Academy Award–winning film *The Shape of Water* includes a musical number during which our mute protagonist Elisa (Sally Hawkins) is suddenly able to sing her heart out. With each fantasy sequence, time slows down, and the characters exit the confines of their ordinary lives for an alternate paradise where everything is finally made right—the lighting changes, the music swells, and the viewers are able to take a deep breath and bask in a vision of the way things are *supposed* to be.

The fantasy sequences depicted on the screen feel so distorted from reality that it took me some time to even recognize the possible overlap with my own thirteen-year-old fantasy sequence scribbled into my diary. How is my vision of a future, walking self any different from Eddie Redmayne playing an aging Stephen Hawking, lifting himself up from his wheelchair to pick up a pen on the floor? The fantasy is held up as some kind of culminating, heart-throbbing moment to capture this character's deepest longing—*if only*, it whispers, hand clutching heart. The amount of screen time, the tone of the music, the altered lighting place these moments on a pedestal that hardly seems comparable to my very ordinary, fleeting childhood daydreams.

More than anything, I see one fundamental difference between these on-screen fantasies and my thirteen-year-old musings—*my* diary dream wasn't wrapped up in having legs that obeyed my every order. I just wanted the kind of story that seemed exclusively available to nondisabled women. I wanted a fun, challenging job. A boyfriend. A cool apartment. I didn't know the girl in the paralyzed body could have that. My fantasy sequence was caught up in a complex social context—a tiny fluff of a moment in the great scope of my life navigating an ableist world. It wasn't about my legs. Nondisabled storytellers don't seem to get that.

This idea that disabled people exist with one sole desire, one holy passion, one desperate fixation on an able body, is overemphasized and obsessively repeated. This doesn't mean there aren't any disabled people who want cures; even people who are pretty content in their disabled bodies sometimes wonder about life with a different body. But it often consumes the character's entire purpose in the plot, with very few alternate narratives to complicate or counter it. It's an old, uninformed, one-dimensional read on disability that burns on the stinky fuel of nondisabled fears.

Maybe one of the most striking, blatant distortions of disability was brought to us by the nondisabled television personality Kylie Jenner in her 2016 photo shoot featured on the cover of *Interview*. Dressed in a black leather bustier and stiletto heels, Jenner sits in a gilded wheelchair with a posture some described as resembling a lifeless sex doll. Jenner's image depicts disability as purely passive, as if her wheelchair is her cage, when in real life, wheelchairs are empowering, liberating tools for so many people. More than anything, I'm amazed by just how many people cosigned this project. Every detail of this image from the early days of its conception to the final execution was curated and crafted by a team of editors, stylists, and photographers. It passed through so many potential gatekeepers who apparently didn't consider what this photo shoot said about the real experiences of actual disabled bodies.

It makes perfect sense, though. Disability appears on screens and magazine pages like an unfamiliar puppet version of real life, because the team telling these stories—the writers, directors, and actors—are almost always only guessing at the reality. They're fumbling in the dark, observing from a distance, trying to make sense of something with their imaginations alone. I'm not interested in making rigid rules—*actors may only represent experiences they've lived!*—but it's important to look at the very loud, destructive, default pattern that has been in the works for years. Disabled folks appear everywhere in our stories but are almost completely rejected from writing rooms, directors' chairs, and acting gigs. The ones being represented are not consulted or included.

The semester I watched *Me Before You* with my students in the disability and literature class, I was stunned by their reactions to the film. When I gasped in horror, they gushed and cooed at the sweet love story. I felt a profound disconnect between our viewing experiences, and I didn't know how to fill the gap. They watched the man in a wheelchair move across the screen, watched him fall in love, watched him decide to end his life—and the images didn't scrape the same tender wounds. They couldn't see what I saw, couldn't feel what I felt. How do you invite another person into a lifetime of moments—a million tiny stings? How do you translate the sharp pain that comes from seeing your secret fears confirmed—that your life really is a tragedy? What words do you choose to communicate the weight of believing—through your spine and into your digits—that you don't belong?

I wish it were possible to take my high school seniors on a field trip to the suburbs of Overland Park, Kansas, in 1999. We'd file down the wrinkled carpet of the narrow hallway to my bedroom and find thirteen-year-old me sprawled across my bed, surrounded by magazine cutouts of airbrushed models. My atrophied legs don't match my muscly arms, my rib cage shapes an asymmetrical trunk, and my knees are scabby from falls and bumps. As I record my dreams in my Anne Geddes diary, they're filtered through the hundreds of vivid stories I've absorbed by my thirteenth year.

On this impossible field trip, we'd take a tour of my earliest memories sitting on the couch in front of *The Little Mermaid* and binge-watching my grandma's recorded stash of *As the World Turns*; we'd observe as I watch hours upon hours of music videos on MTV and every John Hughes film; we'd study my late-nineties obsession with the Spice Girls and Christy Turlington, and we'd chart exactly where I learn which bodies are desirable and which are not, which stories are brought to the center and which are pushed to the margins, who belongs and who doesn't.

I'd point out to them that in my earliest consumption of the stories around me, I instinctually assumed that my story belonged with all the other Real Citizens of Life. Why wouldn't it? I felt like I belonged at the center of my own story. I saw myself alongside Claire Danes and the Olsen twins and Sarah Michelle Gellar. The more time I spent out in the world, though, the harder it was to see myself in that light.

Then we'd travel back to the morning I start kindergarten, and they'd watch as a short yellow school bus pulls up to our house. They'd watch my face when I get on and find myself surrounded by a group of people I don't recognize. I'd expected to ride the bus with the kids I knew would be in my class. *Am I on the right bus? What universe am I in?* But this was the bus designated for the disabled kids, I learned—kids I'd never met and didn't go to school with. Even by the tender age of six, thousands of images of love and femininity, romance and success, independence and power had flashed across my developing brain. None of them looked like this scene before me on the bus, but apparently this was my story.

If my students and I could take this field trip and observe it all unfolding from a distance, I wonder whether they'd be able to track my growing shame, watch me slowly disappear, more and more disconnected from the world and myself.

By the time I reached the age of my students, my diary offered a snapshot of a mind developing in a world that hadn't made space for it. Just like my imagined future with a boy named Nathan and legs that could walk up stairs, I visualized a future body that could slide right into the scenes of adulthood I'd seen performed by Julia Roberts and Meg Ryan. In a world without any pictures pairing success and wheelchairs, cute boyfriends and paralyzed legs, glamour and disabilities, I didn't know how to imagine my disabled body into the stories I found enticing. I knew I was real, knew I had a story to live, knew I wanted love and beauty, excitement and fulfillment—I just needed the body to match.

A lack of representation shaped my perception of a possible future abstractly and broadly but also tangibly and specifically. In a very practical sense, I didn't know what it looked like for a body like mine to be physically intimate with another body—how would we hold hands as we strolled down the street together? How would we embrace at the airport after a long absence? How would we tumble into bed together? I didn't know how a stylish, accessible home looked—what do I do with all that cupboard space I can't reach? What about rugs that catch on my wheels? How do I gracefully carry a coffee cup from my kitchen to my living room without making a giant mess? I didn't know what kind of job I could have—could I really be a teacher? What would it look like for me to command the attention of a classroom when I sit so low to the ground? These are all things I've figured out (mostly—I still spill a *lot* of coffee), but none of them was *shown* to me first. So much of my adulthood—from the big dream to the gritty mechanics—has been about starting from scratch, building from the ground up, and adapting as I go.

I live in a culture that uses my form as a symbol, a shorthand, an illustration for something else—weakness, captivity, and victimization or super strength, triumph, and feel-good inspiration. Even if I do claim a narrative all my own, when I go out in public, I can feel others' stories written all over my body—stories I didn't and would never choose for myself. I feel like I'm speaking the same language but somehow my words get pulled and picked and sorted until they fit into someone else's narrative. Our stories continually reduce disability into something small—a trinket to manipulate—as if an experience as sweeping, rambling, layered, contradictory, ordinary, vibrant, and *human* as disability could be reduced to something so one-dimensional.

And in case this isn't clear, let me emphasize: more is at stake than hurt feelings, irritations, and misunderstandings. Stories written about marginalized people embed themselves in our culture and are used to justify our politics, to arrange our school systems, to determine a hospital's budget. They enter our private homes, follow us into libraries, classrooms, airports, restaurants, courthouses, swimming pools, doctors' offices, churches, bars—these skewed, melodramatic narratives shape our cities, our communities, our social interactions. They precede us, follow us, and are almost impossible to shake. When we arrive at job interviews, go to the grocery store, show up at a fertility clinic or adoption agency, create online dating profiles, get pulled over by police, entrust our bodies to medical professionals, pick up our kids from school, enter a place of worship, we are moving through a world where our image is shorthand for something incompetent or unreliable, helpless or dangerous, not worth living or inherently wrong, sinful or contagious, impotent or taboo, perverted or sexless. And these manifest into tangible results from neglect to hate crimes, condescending laughter to sexual assault, unwelcome prayers to exorcisms, pity to assisted suicides, infantilization to police violence, dismissal to invasive medical procedures, familial rejection to domestic violence, idolization to social isolation.

I get it—movies are entertainment. But these stories connect to thousands upon thousands of personal, painful stories clustered under a very real oppressive social structure backed by the momentum of hundreds of years.

So, yes, let's agree that disabled people are an essential, vibrant part of our world, and they deserve to be treated as such. But if we stop the conversation here—if we think this is all there is—we haven't moved much farther than the "right" answer— *Diversity and inclusion are good! Don't be mean to disabled people!* Inclusion isn't better just because it's kinder. We should bring disabled perspectives to the center because these perspectives create a world that is more imaginative, more flexible, more sustainable, more dynamic and vibrant for everyone who lives in a body.

The undeniable fact is that we all have bodies that make

messes, fluctuate in size, cramp and bloat, rebel and disobey, break and heal, break again and heal all wonky, hurt and age, speak to us, work for us, get tired, grieve, and rejoice—but mainstream narratives tell us that our bodies aren't that complex. They exist in the extremes: thin women who eat greasy cheeseburgers every day but never gain an ounce, badass fighters who roll over the hoods of cars with ease, couples who have simultaneous orgasms in positions anatomically impossible for real sex—*or*, bodies that are devastatingly sick, only fat, and entirely broken. How many of us see ourselves reflected here? Our actual experiences exist in the thousands of spaces between.

Disabled bodies have always been a part of our collective story, whether we acknowledge it or not—and right now, they're a largely untapped reservoir, waiting to add texture and depth, new jokes and plotlines, curiosity and nuance, adaptability and access to our understanding of what it means to live together on this planet. As we reach for narratives that test the boundaries of identity and reimagine the expectations of gender, race, and sexuality, disability is ready to contribute to a conversation that challenges old paradigms and asks new questions about what it means—what it could mean—to be human.

Disability can give us new stories for navigating an ever-changing world. New stories like: *Maybe hard work has its limits. Maybe your efforts aren't the best barometer for predicting your successes. Maybe the state of your body isn't actually the ticket to happiness. Maybe when someone's difference scares you, that's the precise moment to lean in, shut up, and listen. Maybe true love can be tender and caring and steady. Maybe some shit just happens, and it's not for a greater good, but maybe you'll find a way to be okay anyway. Maybe there aren't happy endings, maybe life is more like a bowl of soup flavored with contentment and angst, victories and heartbreaks, joys and defeats, rage and peace, and maybe it's a special thing when you get to share that soup with anyone.* We don't want to include disabled perspectives just because it's nice or fair to the "handicapped" people. We want to weave these stories into the collection, we want to consider disabled folks as worthy of their own, ordinary storylines, because without them, we are less robust, less flexible, and less equipped for the ride we're already on.

So, yes, representation is nothing short of everything.

5

THE PRICE OF YOUR BODY

Tim Taussig got his first job as a bank teller when he was twenty-one years old. He'd just married my mom a few weeks before, and with his early earnings, he purchased a trailer that spanned eight feet by thirty-four feet (counting the hitch). He worked as an employee of this bank for the next forty-three years and eight months. Every single morning I lived with him, from my infancy to adulthood, my dad rose at 4:30 in the morning. He threw on his clothes, sometimes in his sleep, and took a prayer walk through our neighborhood, regardless of snow, rain, or whether or not his babies had been up all night. He came home, took a shower, ate a disgustingly healthy breakfast, combed his hair to the side, put on his suit, and was on his way to the bus that would take him to work by 6:13 (a bus he never missed once). He worked in his office all day, five days a week. No heading in late to work or taking an early afternoon off. I think the man took half a sick day in his entire career, and then, only when his body was protesting with a high fever and hacking lungs. My mom was sure he was dying. Why else would he stay home? He returned each night at 6:17 in time for dinner with his wife and six kids. His unflagging routine felt more constant than the trees growing in our yard or the beams holding up our house.

I watched all this carefully and with growing awe. When I was little, I would wait for him in the front yard, practicing dance routines with my walker as the minutes ticked closer to his return home. As I got older, I'd stir when I heard him leaving the house. I could see the pitch-black night through my curtains. I'd turn over in my bed, and as I fell back asleep, I wondered how he managed to operate in a world where nighttime is your morning. I never wanted him to know how late I'd slept in on a Saturday. When I bumped into him in the kitchen, his T-shirt sweaty from his just having mowed the lawn or his arms full of grocery bags, I'd pretend I'd been up for hours—I had only stayed in bed because I was reading. No decent person would sleep away that much of the day!

While my dad continued his rigid, unwavering routine, I started to miss more and more school. When my CD alarm clock started to blare the *A Walk to Remember* soundtrack at 7 in the morning, I was exhausted and anxious. Lifting my head felt like swimming across a freezing lake. At least once a week, there was a day when I wasn't sure I could manage to get dressed, let alone sit through seven classes. I started to fall behind in school, and the more behind I got, the more I fantasized about living in a cave. I'd pull my comforter over my head and pretend I lived in deep dark solitude. I didn't see a clear or easy reason for these patterns. I didn't have the flu or strep throat or cancer. I just felt ill-equipped for the task at hand.

In the second month of my freshman year of high school, my school counselor called me into her office because I'd been missing so many days of school. "So what's going on?" she asked me. I don't remember her tone, but I know I received it as accusatory. Before she'd finished her question, hot tears were spilling down my cheeks faster than I could wipe them up. "I don't . . . I . . ." The words caught in my chest. I struggled to push them out of my mouth, to take a deep breath. I could hear myself gasping, hear her telling me to breathe, just breathe. She sounded far away, like she was mumbling to me from the next room. My own voice was so much louder—it sounded frantic and high-pitched, but my rational mind couldn't figure out why. *Stop it! Get in line! Just calm down and do the things!* I felt furious with myself for failing to keep up, to manage the basic tasks all my peers seemed so able to handle. I don't remember any of the words I managed to get out, but the counselor talked with my parents, and together they decided I should drop two of my classes and finish out high school with an adapted schedule. I was so relieved, and so ashamed.

Now, in all of my retrospective wisdom, I can dissect my poor attendance to its tiniest particles. Some of my sick days were tied up with the unique pains of my body. At least once a month, my back and side would surge with raging nerve pain that flared every time I spoke or took a deep breath, let alone moved my

whole body. Some of it was surely wrapped up in anxiety and depression. I felt like a glaring typo on the text of my high school,
a clear outsider, the thing that did not belong. I'm certain there
were others who felt this way, too; I just didn't know how to see
them yet. And of course, navigating through a world that doesn't
operate with your disabled body in mind is simply exhausting. I
didn't understand the web of factors pushing me back into bed
day after day. Instead, I just felt like a giant, incompetent failure.

As I got older, I couldn't fathom how I would grow up to
work a Full-Time Adult Job. How would a girl who could barely
get through a week of high school even approximate Tim Taussig's Working Adult Schedule? The contrast between our days
was stark and embarrassing. But there were other, logistical
barriers that made it difficult to picture, too. Like every year on
"Take Your Daughter to Work Day," I tried to ride the public
bus with my dad, and every year, my disabled body seemed to
single-handedly shut down the entire transportation system. The
bus drivers never knew how to work the lifts or attach the extra
strap to lock my wheels to the bus floor. As the years went by, my
peers were getting jobs as waitresses and baristas, landscapers and
grocery-store cashiers, but I couldn't picture myself fitting into
any of these jobs. How could I deliver plates of food to tables? Or
operate espresso machines that rested on countertops I couldn't
reach? And if I couldn't get a job, could I even be an adult?

Even at a very young age, I found it difficult to picture myself
in the future. I couldn't imagine life beyond being my parents'
child with any clarity or practicality. When I was eight or nine,
I started somberly reporting to my parents that I would not live

past the age of fourteen. What a cruel and creepy thing for a kid to say to her parents, right? (Sorry M & D!) But I didn't mean it to be ominous. Honestly, I think it came from an earnest inability to see into my adulthood—my future was a blinding-white blank slate. How would I ever navigate the hoops laid out before me? How would I pay the steep bill attached to living in this body of mine?

Two summers before I graduated from high school, my longtime best friend Bertie and I volunteered with our church to work at a summer camp located a few hours outside of the city. Like most camps, it wasn't accessible. This didn't surprise or even upset me. It was totally what I expected, what I always expected, from the built spaces around me. Plus, Bertie and I were experts at maneuvering the inaccessible. We'd been friends since the early, awkward days of seventh-grade band, sitting side by side playing flute, catching each other's eyes and giggling whenever our ragey director threw another fit. She knew how to tilt my chair to the side whenever I needed to pop my wheel back into place, didn't hesitate to bump me down a flight of stairs whenever they appeared in our path, and didn't get frazzled by a big grassy hill. We always found our own weird way, and I remained relentlessly optimistic that we could make anything work. I applied for the camp counselor position with the caveat that Bertie would do it with me. Together, we would plow through it all, like we did through craft fairs and theme parks and high school hallways.

Within a few weeks, the camp declined my application. Administrators explained in a few words: I wouldn't be able

to fulfill the duties of a counselor, or even an assistant counselor, on their grassy, hilly, covered-in-stairs campgrounds. I
was devastated and pretended I didn't care at all. I was totally
chill, easy breezy, whatever, babe. Bertie suggested we reapply
for positions in the kitchen, and after a bit, the camp came
back with a different answer. Bertie and I could be assistant
cooks in the smallest camp kitchen. After the sting of the initial rejection subsided, we were both thrilled.

We were just as efficient at washing dishes as any typical
high school camp staffer. (So, not *tremendously* efficient.) We
invented games to make washing hundreds of dishes into a good
time and listened to Relient K and Audio Adrenaline as we
plopped canned fruit onto serving dishes. In the afternoons we
ran around with the kids on the rickety playground equipment
and played cards in our little cabin. Bliss.

One afternoon, as Bertie pushed me back to our cabin for
an hour of playing Hearts and chomping on Pringles, she
whispered behind my ear, "I saw something I wasn't supposed
to." I begged her to tell me what it was, but she wouldn't until
the door was closed tightly behind us.

"Have you noticed that we have like a hundred percent more
free time than anyone else working here?"

My mind filed through memories of the past few days: we
were in the kitchen a few hours a day, and the rest of the time,
we wandered around the camp, took naps, and painted each
other's nails.

"Yep." I laughed.

"Well. I saw a sheet of paper that listed the positions of

every single staffer at camp," she said. Her eyes were wide, but I couldn't tell whether she was amused or angry. Maybe both. "And next to each person's name there was a little '1,' like the position was filled with one person. Next to our names?—they put zeros."

In other words and as we reasoned, the camp seemed to have invented these positions for us in order to give us something to do—to make us feel included. (And by "us," I mean me. Of course Bertie could have had a real staff position if she weren't busy helping me over the bumpy campgrounds and up the steps of our cabin.)

Bertie kept talking, and I think I even giggled, but inside? All I could hear was this: *the work you're doing at this camp—your presence here—is comprehensively, quantifiably, undeniably worthless.* Not only was I a zero, but I'd made Bertie a zero as well. I was a burden, taking up so much of Bertie's energies that I robbed her of any worthwhile contributions she could have made.

"Well, at least we know we never have to come back!" I said, trying to stay light and bright. I'd really believed I was contributing something to the camp, holding out my open hands with something of value to offer. But somehow, this contribution didn't fit into the camp's system of tasks and work. Every hour I'd spent spraying down the dirty plates, singing loudly over the dishwasher, opening cans of peaches, giggling with the kids on the playground—every moment that had meant something to me, every memory that was still plump and soft with that sweet camp glow, felt sucked of meaning, like a jelly doughnut scraped into a hollow, bland pastry carcass. My efforts didn't count. Literally. The dismissal made me pull back and clench my hands into tight fists.

As I neared my graduation from high school, I hovered on the edge of what felt like an endless canyon. I couldn't picture how I would survive this endless stretch of landscape, let alone where I fit into it. I knew there were paths that could get you safely from one side to the other—go to college, pick a major that will land you a job, pay your bills, save some money, and retire into the sunset—but no matter how chipper and positive I tried to be, I started to see more and more signs that my body would not glide easily through these mile markers. Each step and turn brought complications, each milestone came with costs. And one fee waiting for me in adulthood would arrive on my twenty-third birthday. As my dad reminded me with increasing urgency, I would be ejected from his health insurance coverage when I turned twenty-three. *Happy birthday!*

I expect this rite of passage is distinctly American. In 2010, the cutoff was extended to one's twenty-sixth birthday. Every once in a while, I find myself playing the impossible "what if?" game, imagining what choices I would have made, what dreams I would have chased, had I grown up in a country where the fear of not having health insurance didn't haunt the background of the possibilities I allowed myself to imagine. Would I have taken more risks, followed my gut, dodged some bullets, breathed more easily if the constant fear of paying for my body were put to the side?

I'd known of this looming twenty-third-birthday deadline

since I was a young girl. Year after year, my chest tightened just a little bit more. I knew I was expensive. For as long as I could remember, I'd been racking up medical bills for my parents with a never-ending string of treatments, visits to specialists, prescription medications, and regular testing. I was also very aware that we didn't have money to spare—we drove our janky, sputtering cars to the ground, wore only hand-me-downs and second-hand clothes, "vacationed" at my grandmother's three-bedroom ranch in Lawrence, Kansas, and splurged by sharing an extra-large pizza at Godfather's on our birthdays. I saw my dad going out of his way to save seventeen cents on milk, even as I sat in a wheelchair that cost more than his car. The older I got, the more I cringed at the bills my body created. It took me a bit longer to realize just how lucky we were. The only reason my parents were able to pay for my body at all was because of the health insurance policy my dad received through his full-time job at the big bank downtown. Many people do not have this kind of coverage or stability.

✳ ✳ ✳

Just after my twenty-second birthday, my anxieties about healthcare rise to an ear-splitting crescendo. The cutoff is nearing when I get off a return flight to Kansas City late on a Tuesday night. I'm driving my truck home from the airport, hyped up on travel adrenaline and airplane Dr Pepper, updating my longtime boyfriend Sam with every detail of my trip. (You know Sam—the kid who bought me a Magic Eye book when we were eight, the one I loved/hated like a brother, eventually married, and very quickly unmarried.) He sits in the passenger seat, giving just enough "mhmmms" to fuel me onward. I'm still chatting when I park my car in front of my parents' house, swing my legs to the side of the car, and prepare to transfer into my wheelchair. I interrupt my own relentless narrating, confused. "I think my legs might be asleep." I scowl down at my entirely lifeless legs, trying not to panic. I pinch them and shake them, but I don't feel even a tingle of blood rushing back to them. My panic rises, and I start to pound my shins and thighs with my fists. "What's going on?" I ask Sam, my voice painfully high and thin.

"Just breathe," he says, lifting me into my chair. "You probably just need to stretch out." He pushes me and my wheelchair into my parents' house, helps me into bed, and rubs my legs with his hands. My parents hover above me with Sam. No one says very much, but everyone stays close and watchful. Sam wipes panic tears off my cheeks, strokes my hair, and murmurs that he's sure everything is fine. That's when I realize I'm sitting in a puddle of my own urine without the smallest sensation that I'd needed to go. Without warning or precedent, I've lost every bit of sensation and function from my waist down.

This news might not sound like an enormous deal if you don't understand a little about how my body functioned before this moment. I mean, the doctors and nurses in the ER seem startlingly unconcerned when we arrive later that night, so here's the quick sketch: From the days when I first started falling when I was three years old to this moment shortly after exiting the plane, I had spotty sensation from my waist down—more feeling in my right leg than my left, more feeling on my inner thighs than my outer. I could stretch my legs and stand for a bit. I could walk short distances by pressing one hand against a wall and holding on to someone's shoulder with the other. I could walk slowly up and down stairs that had a railing. I could stand in the shower if there was something to hold on to. I could lean against the sink while I washed dishes. I could lift my wheelchair in and out of my car by pulling it over my body.

In an instant, all of this is inexplicably gone, like a light switch turned off. I can't feel the slightest pressure or twinge or tingle, even as I dig my fingernails into the skin on my legs. With all my effort and concentration, I can't wiggle a toe, let alone stand. These changes in my body will require a fundamentally different way of interacting with the world—I won't be able to transfer into my car the same way or use the bathroom or the kitchen in my house. I'll need to find a new system for managing my bladder and bowel routines, for hanging out with friends. As soon as I think about sex, I start to cry.

I'm not the first person to find herself in this position. Across the planet, people are making these kinds of adjustments every day, but I'd been under the naive impression that I'd already done all the adjusting the universe would ever ask of me. I've had no warning, not even a whiff of a hint, that these changes were on the horizon, and I'm reeling. Has my cancer come back? Did I get injured without realizing it? Is it only going to get worse?

I spend the night in the ER where they run expensive tests requiring machines that look like they belong in a dystopian future. As they inject dye into my spinal cord and take pictures,

I'm comforted in my belief that somebody, somewhere will be able to tell me what's wrong. In the earliest hours of the morning, they transfer me to the inpatient floor. Lying in my starched, white bed under the searing, fluorescent lights, I meet with neurosurgeons, neurologists, and physical therapists. No one can tell me what happened or why. (And no one has since. It's an incomplete puzzle that I still struggle to put away.)

Without any medical explanation, my sensation starts to return. I wiggle one big toe, then clench a muscle in my right thigh. One afternoon with a room full of visitors, I shout, "I have to pee!" like I just discovered a lifetime supply of chocolate under my hospital bed. Soon after, I'm transferred to a rehab hospital where I live for a week, followed by months of outpatient therapy until my body nearly resembles the body I'd known before. Day after day, my brain tallies the bills. Each time they draw my blood, every doctor who sits with us for three minutes of "consulting," every stool softener nurses bring me in a tiny plastic cup becomes an item on the mile-long-printout bill. If my dad hadn't already met his insurance deductible and out-of-pocket max that year, we knocked it out of the park in the first month. I feel the numbers like a grainy pit in my stomach, but the sour that won't leave my mouth is the cold hard calendar facts: I am unspeakably grateful for my dad's insurance, but I'm turning twenty-three in ten months. What if this had happened a day after I had turned twenty-three? Could I have even paid for the first trip to the ER? What am I going to do?

This is a very personal story, but it's part of a much bigger story, too. So many human beings live under the threatening shadow of health insurance—so many of us have shitty insurance, or pay astronomical prices to have insurance (even when it's shitty), or live in fear of losing our insurance (yes, even the shitty kind). More of us than we'd like to believe live one emergency room visit away from bankruptcy or avoid getting that lump checked because it's probably nothing and who can afford to pay just to be safe? There are those who will be paying off medical bills into old age from the motorcycle accident they had in their early twenties or the open-heart surgery performed on their newborn baby. In case you can't quite tell where I stand on this issue: this is some bullshit. The single most universal trait we all share is having a body, and all of us, no matter what, are susceptible to the frailties of that body. All bodies age, weaken under the power of germs, viruses, diseases, pain, and injury, require intervention and maintenance, rebel and go rogue. All of our bodies are at risk (some much more than others), and there could not be more at stake. This is inescapably true—and yet. Not all of our bodies have the same access to care, and let's be clear: all of our bodies deserve care.

After the initial shock that my body is actually a minefield of instability starts to recede, the days begin to feel more manageable. Sam goes on slow walks with me as I cling to my walker with wild-eyed determination. My sister brings her kids with stacks of homemade cards and little baggies of peach gummies. My mom is there every single day with a bag of books and a notepad where she can keep a record every time a person with a medical degree stops by and says anything. My dad visits in the evenings after work. It's the nights when I'm left with the cold fear that, no matter what I try to do to prevent it or wish it away, any part of my body might stop working at any instant. (This is technically true for all of us, despite the fact that we've collectively agreed to believe the opposite—that with a good diet and exercise, we will live healthily for eternity.) This realization feels just as shocking to me, a young paralyzed woman, as I'm sure it's felt to others in their prime. It's scary to look the facts in the face: my body is vulnerable, impermanent, and only wearing down.

One of my first nights in the inpatient rehab hospital, I sit with my knees propped under my chin and stare at myself in the mirror above the sink, running the tips of my fingers over my shins to verify that I can still feel the edge of my nails. Only one light is on in the room, so my face is marked by sharp shadows. I peer at the girl in that reflection. What good does she have to offer? The purple circles under her eyes and her dull, sallow skin verify to me that I am not healthy or strong, but small and fragile. I decide that I don't trust the girl in the mirror to take care of me. She will never be able to earn the money, pay the bills, afford healthcare for herself. What will she do the next time she is inevitably hospitalized at the age of twenty-four or thirty-two or forty and is no longer on her dad's insurance?

I feel my perception of my body fundamentally shifting. My form feels frail, permeable, unreliable—like parts of it might fall off or crumble to a powdery dust at any moment. Life feels too hard. I can't do this. And right there, curled up in the hospital bed at the age of twenty-two, I decide to give up. I'm not going to try—to find a career or a place in this world, to fight for plans to move out on my own, to pay my own bills, to strive to build a life of my own. I will shred any budding plans I might have had for my life and sink deep into the role of invalid like a warm, lethal bubble bath.

One month after I'm released from the rehab hospital, Sam proposes, and six months later, we get married. It feels like more than a good idea; it feels inevitable. Despite the fact that we spent the preceding five years of dating nearly breaking up every other month, I can't imagine another way forward. Also, Sam recently started a full-time job. It comes with health benefits, and he can put me on his coverage if I'm his wife. I feel safe.

✳ ✳ ✳

At the time, I didn't think about our marriage in those terms—*I will marry this person, even though we're not terribly compatible and he kind of annoys me, because I want to have health coverage.* When I reflect on it now, it's difficult to untangle the messy mass of reasons that I married Sam, let alone how I made sense of it at the time. Sam's love for me felt like a great fluke, a crack in the laws of the universe, and if I didn't jump at the chance for romance, that would be it—poof! *No love for you!* I was terrified of the big wide world, and Sam felt so safe and steady. Maybe I confused relief for love, support for intimacy, security for compatibility? We'd been friends since we were eight years old, and between the two of us, we'd gathered a roaring bonfire of shared memories.

Almost a decade later, I have a difficult time looking squarely at these reasons. To be honest with you, I'm holding my breath as I type these words out, because I don't like to look at them. I feel more regret, embarrassment, and shame about my decision to marry Sam than almost any other in my life. (Because, as you very well know, this marriage did not go well, and as you might have guessed, not only did I make a magnificent mess of everything on my way out of it, but I ended up hurting Sam in a big way.) It's easy for me to slip into a dark spiral when I confront my willingness to use another person for my own sense of safety. I hate that I did that. I wish I could go back and redo it.

But there's another voice in my head, too. She's like the grandmother of us all and speaks from a place above the sloppy heap of guts and tears. (Maybe she's the haggard one I saw in the mirror that night.) She reminds us: I made this decision as a young twenty-two-year-old. And perhaps more important, I was a young twenty-two-year-old trying my very best to stay alive without a clue how to do it. I didn't have any practical support from a community that had navigated this path before, knew the roadblocks and bends, and could point me to wells and shaded areas.

This is one of the profound consequences of having an identity you don't share with the living, breathing community around you—your family and friends, teachers and mentors. When you're born into a marginalized community whose members share your identity, you are born into a family that understands and knows. They've been through the same things. They carry the insider knowledge, and they can help prepare you. (There are other complications and particular abuses attached to those who are born into a community with shared oppression, but collective insider knowledge seems to be a unique gift, as well.) People with disabilities are usually born into families that don't share their disability or know anything about the world they live in. Family members can learn, but they're starting from scratch. I didn't know anyone who'd navigated their own adulthood from a disabled body, and I'd never seen it depicted meaningfully on a screen or a page. I'd never talked with a disabled woman about falling in love or how she chose her partner, didn't know any inter-abled couple who could model or describe this part of their relationship, had never heard anything about programs that might have helped me find a job or get some health insurance. In my universe, this was the Wild West, and I was the only cowboy of my kind, trying to live on drips of water from a prickly cactus.

* * *

Soon after Sam and I marry, I reckon with a very harsh truth about myself: the instability of being uninsured, unemployed, and alone does not feel as overwhelming, incapacitating, or defeating as being partnered with the wrong person. I move out of our house six months after I moved in.

I say this now like it was an easy choice. It wasn't. It was a time of turmoil, grief, anger, destruction, reckoning, and healing. It was scary and exciting, and in my desperation—for good or for bad—I did things I never imagined I could do.

In the middle of this catastrophic exit I accidentally learn a bit of insider knowledge: if you are disabled enough and poor enough in the United States, you qualify for monthly Social Security checks and Medicaid benefits. The very first I hear of this is from a disabled friend of a friend who comes home for a visit over fall break. Instead of catching up with my friend, I soak up every bit of information and solidarity I can glean from this real-life disabled woman who looks like me and moves like me and navigates the world with the same set of barriers I encounter every day. In my entire life, no one has told me about these programs—not my doctors or teachers or school counselors. How did this vital information fall through the cracks? Why didn't they know?

Researchers at Cornell University looked at data gathered in 2017 and found that while about 65 percent of nondisabled people get their health insurance through their employers, 66 percent of disabled folks receive health coverage through Medicaid or Medicare. But qualifying for government healthcare is contingent on remaining poor. In other words, in order to have health insurance, a lot of disabled people are forced to choose between hovering near the poverty line or trying to find and survive a full-time job that accommodates their bodies and includes health benefits—a unicorn within the disabled community, where fewer than one in four people is employed full-time. With this setup, the relentless need for good health insurance can shape major life decisions for those who live in bodies that require regular medical care.

So after growing up with the fear that I'd surely die as soon as I became an adult, after making reckless, frantic decisions I thought would keep me safe, one of my worst fears about my future is abruptly quelled. I have no job, no experience or references or degrees to get a job, no bank accounts, no prospects, and still—I feel like I've won every prize. My Medicaid card pays for every appointment with every specialist, every medication I depend on, every test my doctors order. I breathe in freedom and exhale peace. I'm going to be okay.

The good news is that I'm so broke, I also qualify for subsidized housing set aside for folks sixty-three and older—and/or those with disabilities (that's me!). I'll never understand how it happened so fast, but a unit becomes available for me just a month after I put my name on the waiting list. I move into the ground floor, corner apartment in a building populated with people who remind me of my grandma and some of her crankiest friends. They watch from their third- and fourth-floor apartment windows to make sure I get home safely at night and berate anyone who dares to park in my spot by the back door. I get on food stamps and proudly purchase eggplant, cereal, soymilk, and eggs from the Aldi down the street. For a while, this tiny little world, measured out in monthly Social Security disability checks of $674, feels like my very own fairytale kingdom. I finish up my bachelor's degree with help from vocational rehabilitation services, and the amount of my disability checks slowly decreases as I start to earn a bit of my own money. For years, I live well below the poverty line on a small stipend for teaching English classes while I make my way through graduate school. My world is small, but as long as I don't move too suddenly in any direction, the waters remain still. I'm okay.

Surprise! Soon, it becomes more complicated. After a few years in graduate school, I take on a little part-time job working an additional five to eight hours a week at the center for teaching on campus. I want this job because it's a great place to learn more about teaching, and I think it'll be nice to have just a tad more money to buffer those stretches between checks. As soon as I take on this new, modestly paid position, however, my monthly income edges into ineligible-for-benefits territory. I start finding notices nearly every month that they've overpaid me—I actually *owe* money—so, I write checks every month to even out the balance. All the while, I keep a vigilant eye on my bank account. If I try to save any extra money, I run the risk of crossing the line and losing benefits.

With the tiny bit of extra income, I decide I might be able to move into a little house with Bertie—a decade after our days playing flute together in the middle-school band, she still isn't afraid to bump me down a flight of stairs or, apparently, go on a house-hunting quest with me. I've loved living with the senior citizen rat pack, but I also feel lonely. I live on an island where me and my sixty-three-and-older pals have 4 a.m. tea parties to watch royal weddings, but I also feel isolated from people my age. I try to work it out; I might be able to afford splitting the rent on a cheap house. If I can maintain the balance of earning a little more, affording a little more, and keeping my benefits? It's a tightrope, hold-your-breath, no-sudden-moves, fingers-crossed fling at living my life.

As soon as I start looking for a different place to live, I realize I'm terrified of crossing state lines and losing my Medicaid benefits. I live right on the edge of Kansas bumping against Missouri, but all of the options on the Missouri side are attached to the risks of having to reapply, of waiting months for the paperwork to be processed, all the while with no coverage and no guarantee of support at the end of the process.

I want to speak with someone who can talk me through the best steps to take when moving and trying to cause as little disruption as possible to my Medicaid benefits. I've never steered my ship through these waters; I need someone to guide me. I don't have a great history accessing this kind of information from Social Security, but I want to take my fate by the horns! Surely, there's a better way—I just need to barrel through and make it to the other side.

I phone Social Security and wait on hold for more than an hour. When I finally hear a human voice, the woman on the line is immediately combative, even as she asks me simple questions like my name and Social Security number. She stops talking for minutes at a time without any explanation, and I wonder whether she is typing or has left for her lunch break. About ten minutes in, I realize I'm nauseous. My heart is pounding. About fifteen minutes in, I have yet to ask the question that's prompted the call. I frantically draw flowers on my notepad. When we finally arrive at the moment—it's time to ask the question, and hopefully get that coveted information!—I rush through the rehearsed inquiry. Is there any way to easily transfer my benefits from Kansas to Missouri? Is it more likely that I'll be approved in Missouri, since I was approved in Kansas? She pauses. Then accuses me of having two identities. (Are you confused? Same.) She never even approximates an answer to my questions, but she does refuse to hang up the phone first, so I won't be able to respond to the automated survey prompted at the end of every call.

To be fair, this is easily the worst phone call I've ever had with the Social Security Administration. Most of the people I speak with are polite, if pretty unhelpful. Like the woman who happily claims she is helping me sign up for a Working Healthy program; it's only months later, on the phone with another Social Security employee, when I discover she most definitely signed me up for absolutely nothing. The vast majority of time I spend on the phone with Social Security is spent on hold, or with people who tell me the department I actually want to talk with is [*name any other department here*], or pressing numbers for different menus that always lead to dead ends with no human voices.

These conversations are surreal, and I carry them with me every time I consider picking up the phone, reaching out for guidance, or seeking information from Social Security. It's interesting—isn't it?—that the programs put in place to help disabled people afford to live in their bodies are so difficult to find, navigate, or understand, like an oasis surrounded by trap doors, snapping alligators, and guards shouting confusing accusations.

Eventually, Bertie and I find a place to live (another story for another chapter!), and I finish out my graduate degree, while teaching a couple of classes and working my part-time campus job. I continue to perform the delicate dance between not saving too much and affording rent, going after paid writing gigs and not earning too much. By the end of graduate school, I'm very proud—and very tired.

The little girl who grew up staring wide-eyed at her full-time working father leaves graduate school seeing herself as someone who might finally have something to contribute—something unique, important, and needed in the larger world. After being a student as long as they'll possibly let me, I'm ready to go out into the world and finally start adulting. I try to conjure my perfect job into being. Something with writing and teaching and people and flexibility and joy and books and creativity and curiosity! I'm ready! But with every job I consider, I'm forced to review the life-or-death tightrope before me. I need to find a job that either earns a low enough salary that I can continue to receive Medicaid OR comes with excellent medical benefits. Very quickly, finding a job that matches my passions and personality doesn't seem like the most pressing factor. First and foremost: I have to find a way to pay for this body of mine.

When I first see the job posting for a position teaching high school English at a small, independent school, I scroll past it. I hated high school myself, and not just because adolescence is painful. The pace itself exhausted me. I can't picture myself thriving under that relentless speed. When would I write? When would I sleep? When would I pee?

After a month of searching for the unicorn job that would meet my tightrope requirements, I'm exhausted, anxious, and more convinced than ever that the job I want doesn't exist. The high school teaching job pops up again, and I think, "Maybe I could swing it?" I love teaching, love writing, love talking about books, and love my teenage nieces and nephews. The salary is on the lower side for a Full-Time Adult Job (and this much education). It's also three times more than I've ever, in my entire life, made in a year. And—drum roll, please!—it comes with some hearty health benefits.

When I take this job, my first Full-Time Adult Job ever, a feeling rises to the surface. Knowing that my hours of work are officially measured as "full time," knowing that I'll no longer need extra help from the government, knowing that I'll be earning a salary makes me feel so much pride. I feel valuable, worthwhile, respectable, like I've finally earned a "1" next to my name—evidence that I bring more than I take. *I've made it! This is the thing I thought I'd never be able to do, and I'm doing it!*

Before this moment, I had no idea these ideals were lurking just beneath the surface. I didn't know how good it would feel to fit into the standard (ableist) equation of worth: Hours + Production + Wages = Value. This equation is loud, powerful, and everywhere. Those of us who don't work as many hours, who don't "produce" as much (whatever that means), whose wages are lower, or (gasp!) rely on others to survive—we are categorized as a drain, a burden. This ableist model tells us that the human body is a work machine whose value is determined by its production—like a toaster that can toast six slices of bread instead of just the usual two. The more you do, the more hours of overtime you work, the less sleep you get, the more duties you fulfill, the faster you get the work done, the less help you require, the more you're worth.

In the early twentieth century, those with physical disabilities received a "PH" (Physically Handicapped) stamp on their work records, not too unlike the zero placed next to my name during my summer as a camp "staffer." To many employers a "PH" translated easily into "unemployable" or "not worth the trouble," regardless of the job being offered or the precise manifestation of that ambiguous "PH." So here we are, well into the twenty-first century, and how do we assert our inherent worth and value as disabled citizens of the world? So often, I see us try to play by the rules that weren't made for us, try to fit, mask our needs, ignore our bodies, and push harder, harder, harder to prove that we have something to offer. We throw ourselves into the belly of the beast, the very force calling all of the most punishing shots.

Without actually having the tangible "PH" label attached to me, I still feel it as I start my new teaching job—sprinting, striving, committing all of my brain and heart and soul and time and energy to being the Best Teacher Ever. But you guys, being a teacher is *hard*. A lot of full-time working gigs are hard, but this is what I've learned about teaching: it will consume anything you allow it to touch—every cell in your body, piece of your brain, corner of your heart, minute of your waking life. I forget to drink water or avoid drinking water so I won't have to leave a class or a conference or a meeting or a good conversation with my co-workers to go to the bathroom. I stay at school late, take work home, grade all weekend, develop lesson plans in my sleep, forget how to talk about things that aren't related to teaching, become a horrible partner, stop seeing my family, and forget I have a body.

The school cafeteria is located across the campus and always crowded unless you perfectly, precisely time when you get there. I dread the exercise of trying to balance a glass of water and a bowl of soup on the tray resting on my lap in front of my students while trying to make easy-breezy conversation with my colleagues every day. I don't have the emotional space to face that challenge every twenty-four hours, so I start eating handfuls of almonds and protein bars at my desk in between classes. The school notices my absence from the cafeteria and expresses concern, but their attention feels like a reprimand. I hear that I'm making things complicated. They offer to send someone to bring me my lunch every day. I just want everything to settle, don't want to alarm anyone, don't want to make a thing out of this, so I agree for a few months. The most delightful man brings me Styrofoam containers of soup and grilled cheese, nachos, and mac and cheese every day, and we talk about the possibility of snow and his wife who makes warm winter hats and how excited we are for Friday, but eventually, the guilt takes over; I can't ask this man to leave his post in the cafeteria and walk across campus (in the winter!) to bring me a meal every single day. And anyway, I'm never able to finish all the portions they bring me, and I don't want to waste food day after day or leave our office smelling like enchiladas every afternoon. I go back to the almonds.

Within two months of starting the teaching gig, I develop a searing, burning pain running down my left leg. A few months later, my lower back starts aching and throbbing. A few months after that, my legs start clenching and spasming so severely that eventually, I can't unclench them. I try to stand, and my left leg jerks backward, my heel pressing into my bum. Eventually my right leg won't straighten either. As soon as I get into bed each night, my body snaps into the fetal position, like a marionette controlled by a force entirely outside of myself—I can't physically pry my body into an easy, relaxed position. When I sit up in the morning, the pain radiating through my lower back and down into my legs takes my breath away.

And yet, I feel guilty taking days off. I feel silly writing "back pain" into the little window on the substitute teacher request form. I picture the badass lady in the office reading the words— "back pain"—and chuckling. *Yeah, we all have back pain, honey.* I picture my dad taking only half a sick day in his forty-three years of work. I grew up to believe that only negligent, lazy employees ask for sick days unless they literally can't dress themselves and get to work. Technically I can get out of bed, get dressed, and out the door. I'm slower and need help to pull up my pants, but this is my new normal. I will show them I'm not a burden. I'm the "PH" with something to offer. I wasn't a bad hire. I will bring more than I take.

* * *

I write this like it's something that happened a while ago—in the distant past—but this story is still unfolding in real time. Every Monday through Friday, I put on my Adult Working Lady costume. Most days, I think I pass. I keep up, manage, do the tasks (sometimes really well, even), and have good days. I might be getting a little better at putting in for a sick day, at giving 90 percent to a task that used to take 120 percent of me.

At the same time, my body is constantly reminding me: *this system was not made for us.* My body is exhausted, stretched, strained, worn down by the speed and pace and particular demands of being a Full-Time Working Woman—in regular ways

most of us feel, but also in the ways unique to my specific disabilities. I've lost mobility since I started this job. I've developed
a cyst between two vertebrae in my lower back that has invited
new levels of pain and spasticity in my body. I've put extra levels
of strain on my organs. I feel it from my swollen feet to the twitch
of my right eye. I've gotten UTIs, started taking more pain meds
and getting steroid injections into my spine to force my body to
relent and obey. What a brutal trade-off.

I'm torn, because being disabled and having any job at all is a
gift that defies statistics—that counters the very real lived experience of so many folks with bodies that don't fit. I don't want to
fritter away that gift or express ingratitude for being invited to
participate. Nor do I want to suggest that many employers (mine
included) wouldn't do whatever is required to accommodate my
disabled body. So why don't these "special accommodations" feel
more empowering? Why do they remain so hard to swallow?

For starters, there's a contradiction between saying a workplace
is inclusive even as it participates in the larger cultural values that
celebrate everything a disabled body is not. There's something
unsettling about offering accommodations for an "exceptional"
body when the entire system surrounding that body is built on
the assumption that more and faster and harder and higher is
fundamentally, inherently superior. When you applaud your employees *only* for arbitrary measurement of work—arriving early,
leaving late, never taking sick days or time off, or showing up
on the weekend—when you *always* push for *more*—production,
happy hours, publications, softball teams, cases, meetings, tasks,
involvement, spirit, extra—you do not demonstrate an apprecia-

tion for those who have a need, who say no, enforce boundaries, or require flexibility—the very stuff of accommodations masked under different names.

In some ways, "special accommodations" insist that the current setup is just fine, thanks. They cling to the idea that only a few outliers can't fit into the mold, ignoring the fact that even those who can make it work might be better off with a more flexible model. The very notion of "*special* accommodations" relies on the belief that really, there are only a few who don't slip easily into the narrow mold of a nine-to-five schedule, five days a week (clock in! clock out!), getting "sick" only a specific number of times each year, recovering from giving birth and being ready to separate from a newborn baby in a predetermined set of days. So many of us agree to these rules, even as we know we don't thrive there. We're rewarded when we fit tidily into the parameters set before us, so we pretend, mask, and go along with it as best we can. Those who simply cannot fit are highlighted as outsiders who need something extra to make it work. Instead of looking at the larger, varied collection of humans on a team and creating a structure that accounts for their real experiences, needs, desires, and motivations, so often work systems prefer to dispense the smallest portions of flexibility to the ones who simply cannot fake it any longer (or put up the biggest fit and have a lawyer to back them up). I'm glad employers are required by law to dispense those small portions of flexibility. It's an *invaluable* change. It's also entirely limited by the larger environment— the larger cultural values surrounding work and the people in charge—that houses it.

When a system rolls its eyes at those who don't "pull their weight," then offers to lighten their load, you don't trust it. These practices are at odds with "accommodations" and create a confusing, shameful space to work out what it means to take care of your body. Accommodations may be offered in this kind of environment, but they aren't categorized as admirable; they're a last resort, an unfortunate option, a generous gift bestowed upon the ones who regrettably need something. How many employees feel safe asking for something that seems to diminish their value in the eyes of the people evaluating them?

The needs of my disabled body seem clearer. People see me in my wheelchair, and they expect accommodations will follow closely behind (although most don't usually imagine much beyond elevators and ramps). But I believe this Full-Time Working Adult system punishes many more bodies than just mine—bodies in pain, bodies swaddled in depression and anxiety, bodies that get pregnant, need to breastfeed, have periods, get cramps and headaches, bodies that move and process slower than others, have different eating rhythms, need naps, breaks, longer toilet times, more inclusive toilet spaces—and so the list unfurls. A system that measures our worth by an arbitrary amount of work that our bodies and minds are supposed to be able to produce within narrow parameters of time and space punishes all of us. We all eventually sag under its unsustainability.

Why are we so enamored with this vision of Hard Work before and above any other model? I think we've built our understanding of work on an unquestioning faith in a twisted version of "survival of the fittest." We've misunderstood this phrase to mean, *Whoever is strongest, whoever competes the best, whoever works harder than anyone else, whoever is willing to be the most aggressive wins!* But not even Darwin himself touted "survival of the fittest" as the guiding principle of evolution. The species that survived through the unexpected twists and turns over the long haul were the most *adaptable* species, like the peppered moth. During the Industrial Revolution, factories in England polluted surrounding wooded areas. They covered the region with gritty black soot, and lichen-covered trees that were once white were now dark. An entire species of moths that had survived before the soot were now at risk with this unexpected turn. The pale wings that once camouflaged them against the lichen made the moths easy targets against the sooty backdrop. Within this species were a number of darker, "peppered" moths. While their light-winged peers were more at risk, the peppered moths were perfectly suited for the change in environment, and their unusual trait was the very thing that guaranteed their species' survival.

If disabled bodies did nothing else for the human race (which of course, they do), they would ensure our variety, and by extension, our adaptability. We're in the middle of a transition right now, not terribly unlike the shift brought about by the Industrial Revolution. For a while, we've been covering our ears, putting our hands over our eyes, and singing loudly over the reality that so many of us have no easy method of paying for these bodies of ours. More than ever, we need to be adaptable, flexible, and imaginative, but this, right here, is an invaluable perspective the disabled person has to offer: we have our thumbs on the heart-beat of adaptability, we know how to imagine a more flexible world; our very existence, our everyday lives, are an exercise in imagination. We are surrounded by reminders that all our bodies have limits and thrive in different environments. The world we've built, by and large, ignores this. I can't help but wonder: What might happen in all of our work spaces if we put aside the make-believe prototypical worker we inherited from the Industrial Revolution and brought the disabled body to the center?

We already know what we can gain from hard work. My dad is a testament to this gift. Me and my siblings were safe and secure in the little nest he built for us. He devoted the majority of his waking hours in his twenties, thirties, forties, fifties, and part of his sixties toward protecting this. We had food; a house with heat, water, and electricity; and insurance that guaranteed we would be cared for when we got strep throat or cancer. These are certainly gifts many people don't have (even those who are out there working very hard). Now that I'm older, though, I wonder how much my dad lost in his unwavering commitment to that job. He had so many children to support, one of them sick and disabled, and a wife with a kidney disease—did he ever let himself entertain the idea of switching careers? Was he ever dreaming of a different life when his alarm clock blared him awake at 4:30 in the morning for the nine-hundredth day in a row? Maybe he did but was too scared to risk the security this setup gave us. As a child, I never considered this, but as I worked on this chapter, I called him and asked him, "Did you ever worry about losing your job at the bank?"

"Oh, I was terrified," he said. He is matter-of-fact in his delivery, as you might imagine. It wasn't a dramatic confession, but a simple statement of fact. "I had no idea how I would take care of you all if I didn't have that job." Growing up, I never picked up on a whiff of the fear he was holding. He was only ever the steady, stoic Tim Taussig I'd known since the womb. He didn't exist outside the rhythm of working at the bank. But, you guys. He retired on February 25, 2016, and the man has been made new. He's chatty on the phone, he watches shows with my mom, his movements are light, he takes every one of his children (all six of us), their partners (make that another six), and grandchildren (the latest count is twenty-four) out for lunch on their birthdays. I hadn't really noticed his absence before, but now that he's here, I feel his presence.

My dad was my first, most formative picture of Work. He embodied everything the prototypical worker is expected to be. But I have to wonder what parts of himself he would have been able to keep and nourish, how he might have flourished, if he'd been allowed a more imaginative structure. I can almost see it—a world where the breathing, bleeding, exhausted, stretched, and strained human body is invited into the circle, allowed to exist in all its variant forms. What flexibility, what efficiency, what connections, what salves might we find there?

6

FEMINIST POOL PARTY

I hated going to birthday parties when I was little. Especially the sleepover kind. The invitation would arrive in the mail two weeks before, and my mom would put it straight on the fridge. An invitation means you're included, right? And who doesn't want that? But the small paper invite with cartoon girls dancing beneath aggressively bright balloons and riotous pink confetti haunted me, reminding me what was looming ahead. *Samantha is eight! Join us for pizza and swimming and relentless little-girl screaming into the wee hours of the morning!* I begged my mom to make up excuses so I wouldn't have to go.

Parties were vivid reminders that I didn't fit. When I saw the sparkly balloon dancers on the fridge, I imagined all the girls from my class sharing lip gloss in the van waiting to go to the pool while the birthday girl's dad slowly bumped me down the front stairs (*What do I say to a DAD? Where do I look?*). I saw all the girls jumping on each other in the water, easy and light, graceful and wild. I saw myself trying to act casual and chill, gripping the edge of the pool. I saw myself frantically rushing through my nighttime bathroom routine while all the girls waited in a line outside the door, knocking every so often, "Are you okay in there Bekah?" I saw all their cute jammies with tiny ruffles on the sleeves next to me in my giant T-shirt with the rip up the side (it was so soft, though!) and big sister's gym shorts hanging down to my knees. I saw all their fairy feet and delicate ankles next to my swollen toes. (Should I cover them with socks? But no one else is wearing socks to sleep!) I saw myself skipping soda with pizza, terrified I'd wet my sleeping bag during the night. I saw myself pretending to fall asleep in my spot next to the wall while the girls sang along to *Grease 2* and stayed up talking about the boys in our class.

Not being invited *at all* came with a distinct bite, but an invitation meant that I would need to contort myself into a role that never seemed to fit, an exercise I found to be—more than anything else—exhausting. And after all that effort, I still usually left the party feeling like a drag on all the good party times. The girls screaming in the pool had something beautiful. I didn't want to disrupt or pollute that. It was plain to see they were better off without waiting on the one bumping down the stairs with a dad, without having to worry about the one clinging to the edge of the pool. I could try to pretend, but it felt crystal clear: I didn't belong. This, I believed, was a fact—spoken from on high, the hand the universe dealt, the way things were and would be. It never occurred to me that there could or should be a different way.

I wish these feelings were specific to my childhood, memories to marvel at like an artifact from the distant past. But even now, there are plenty of days I feel my thirty-plus self transform into eight-year-old Rebekah, ready to withdraw for the sake of the group.

✳ ✳ ✳

Like always, Micah and I are late to the party, but the hosts meet us at the bottom of the stairs and help Micah lift me up two flights. I grip his forearm as we ascend and give him a squeeze. It says, *I'm glad you're here with me.* This is our first time visiting our friends' loft, and I feel cared for beforehand when they text us ideas for navigating its less inaccessible entrance. This old warehouse was only recently converted into hip, open-floor lofts with the original brick walls and cast-iron beams still on display. *So cool!* I'm wearing my new, black ankle boots that hide the scarred part of my feet, my favorite-fitting, black jeans that have some stretch to hug my tiny legs and pull up over my soft tummy, and the slouchy tee reserved for occasions when I really want to look great without looking like I'm trying to look great. These are the friends who look like they lounged out of a dreamy ad campaign—effortlessly lovely. Do you have these friends, too? I take obnoxious amounts of time getting ready before we hang out with them. When we get to the top of the stairs, I hike up my black jeans, pulling them above the deep crease they're making in my belly.

We're handed fizzy mojitos with freshly muddled mint as we

pass through the front door. I give Micah my feeling-fine-and-fancy look, and the ice tinkles in our glasses as we trail behind our tour guide through the narrow hallways. "Do you think they have any accessible units?" I ask Micah, starry-eyed and impressed by the high ceilings and big windows. He shoots me a skeptical look. "Maybe even just a first-floor unit?" We pass the small bathroom on the way back to the kitchen, and I make a note to slow down on my fluid intake; there's no way I'll be able to get into that bathroom, let alone have a safe pee with a mojito buzz on.

A group of our friends are gathered around a coffee table of treats, lounging on the sofa and sitting on the floor, backs against a cement wall. I stay in my wheelchair and cross my legs, staying put in my designated accessible spot. I never look more disabled than when I try to move from here to there without my wheelchair, and I'm suddenly not feeling in the mood to expose that vulnerability on this posh set of dazzling people.

I'm sipping my mojito and glancing down at my phone, fruitlessly scrolling through the building's website for first-floor units (and quickly realizing I'd never be able to afford this place even if they had a space I could access, which they definitely do not), as I pick up on an animated conversation.

"God, I wish I would have told him to fuck off," Ryan says, shaking his head, his arm draped over his wife Beth's shoulder.

"It wouldn't have made anything better," Beth says. "I mean, you have to imagine the level of creep in a person who thinks it's okay to yell at a woman across a parking lot just because she's wearing yoga pants. And honestly? It happens all the time. I'm used to it." She's brushing it off, like she's bolstered by calluses she's built from a lifetime of being catcalled by male strangers.

The other women in the room emphatically roll their eyes with her, and the men listen. I nod vigorously.

"I've just started hollering back," Grace says, her eyes sparking. "The other day, this guy started following me around the grocery store, muttering nasty things to me, and I was like, 'No. You say that so *everyone* can hear you! So your girlfriend in aisle *five* can hear you! Say that again, loud and proud!'" She reenacts the scene, and the other women are laughing knowingly, in solidarity. It sounds cathartic.

The other two women in the circle share catcalling stories of their own, and each narrative is met with a supportive cloud of understanding murmurings. I throw in phrases like "Wow," and "Good for you! That's some bullshit!"

One of the boyfriends asks, "If there was one thing you really wish men understood about this, what would it be?"

Grace is quick to answer. "The thing men don't understand is—this happens *all the time*." The other women nod vigorously. "Every single woman I know could tell you countless stories just like these. Seriously, ask *any* woman."

"Mmm," I affirm, the only woman in the circle who hasn't added a story to the collection.

And just like that, I'm eight-year-old Rebekah at the sleepover. The distance I feel between Them and Me isn't intentional, and it isn't just a result of staircases and narrow doorways to inaccessible bathrooms—it's so much more complicated than overt hostility or tangible practicality.

I know what it's like to be yelled at across a parking lot, but my stories don't seem to match with these catcalling anecdotes. If I were to tell my version of a man hollering at me—frantically yelling "DON'T FALL!" across a parking lot—the group would droop or scoff or laugh at the absurdity. They might go quiet, or ask questions, or even try to understand, but the circle of solidarity would disappear. Because this is a different conversation. It doesn't seem to fit here. And I don't want to disrupt this cathartic, healing moment they seem to be having.

Micah and I don't stay long at the party. Eventually I have to pee (see: mojitos), and I'm tired. As we drive away from the pretty loft, I swat away a painful, familiar question: Do I belong? I mean, in the fullest sense—do I fit in the circle of Women?

I know, what a silly question. Plenty of signs point toward "yes," right? Like, I use "she" and "her" pronouns. I express myself with props and gestures considered traditionally feminine (like dresses and mascara, crossing my legs and playing with my hair). I nursed my baby dolls when I was little and continued to play with dolls until I was worried my friends would find out (and even then, I kept putting them on my birthday wish list). But when it comes to fitting in with the group? Sharing the memories and feelings and quintessential plights that are said to belong to all women? The fears and joys that bind "us women" together? I often don't relate.

The representative Woman of the Twenty-First Century is tired of being sexually objectified and confined to a few narrow roles. She doesn't want the world assuming she's here only to become a man's wife and have his babies. She wants options and her own storylines and every variety of autonomy and independence and equal pay! I want all of this, too. And also.

I remember my parents' constant battle to keep my sister in "modest" clothes, warning her that she didn't know "how boys look at girls." But they didn't really worry about my wardrobe. I remember going shopping and admiring her body in the dressing room. The shape of her hips in a silky dress or her tiny waist taking up so little space between her crop top and the top of her jeans. I got it. My body didn't tempt like hers or Jennifer Aniston's or the magazine models taped to the inside of boys' lockers. It didn't need to be covered to avoid tantalizing. I didn't have to worry about being modest. Why didn't that feel like freedom?

I remember the older guy at the bookstore approaching me and my sister. "Excuse me," he said, looking at her, "I just can't help but say, you really should be a model. You're so thin, just stunning." My gentle and exquisite sister, already well-acquainted with the male gaze at the age of sixteen, tried to deflect. "I think Bekah should be a model!" she said, stroking my hair. "*She's* stunning." I looked away. At the age of fourteen, I already knew what was coming next. The guy wasn't deterred. "No, you're thinner. You're just *gorgeous*." (I had to dig up my angsty teenage diary to fact-check this memory. I thought time had surely exaggerated the exchange. Turns out, the year 2000 had bold creeps, too.) Did I wish that man had aimed his attention at me? Not exactly. Did I cherish my escape from his attention? I didn't. Did I envy his assessment of my sister? Absolutely. What does that mean?

I remember sitting around a campfire at age fifteen with Sam, his brother, and the girl they both had a crush on. I'd grown my hair out long, because I'd heard Sam liked long hair. The girl had her guitar resting on her thigh, and she sang song after song at the bidding of the boys. The only song I remember is "Kiss Me" by Sixpence None the Richer. When she finished, she turned to me and said, "You know that feeling—when a boy looks at you, and you just know he wants to kiss you?" I stared back with a goofy grin. "No," I said with a breathy giggle in front of the girl with the guitar and the two boys I was certain wanted to kiss her. I laughed, I think, because it felt better than pausing over the embarrassing fact she'd conjured into the circle—apparently, I was the only girl who didn't know the look of a boy who wants to kiss her.

As I've gotten older, more and more of the women in my life have transformed into mothers. I have two sisters and three sisters-in-law who each have between three and seven children. (Yeah, it's a whole thing—Taussigs and their babies.) When my sisters talk about fighting morning sickness, whether to Pitocin or not to Pitocin, Ergobaby versus Babybjörn, weaning and baby weight, I find myself relating more to my twelve-year-old nephew and his dramatic retelling of seeing a coyote in his backyard last night than the women around me.

For a long time, I've said I don't want kids, but the more complicated truth is, I don't know whether I can have kids; I can't trace where my desires end and my coping mechanisms begin. When women have conversations about pregnancy, choice is so often at the center, as it should be. Choice is everything. I also don't know how to begin to untangle the relationship between me, motherhood, and choice. Just how much of my childlessness comes down to something as intentional, precise, and definitive as a Yes or No *choice?* With the exception of nursing my baby dolls when I was a kid, I've never been able to picture myself as a mother. But is that because the examples of disabled mothers I've seen in my life have been few and recent? Or am I really not a very maternal person? I've never been with someone I'd want to parent with before Micah, but even if I can and we do (which feels pretty extraterrestrial at this point), my experience will be different from that of the women I know—it will exist outside the picture of pregnancy and labor and mothering that's somehow touted as "standard." My choices will be of a different set.

To add to it all, there will be those who believe I'm not fit to be a parent as soon as they see my wheelchair, and just like people assume Micah is my caregiver or my sibling but rarely my partner, there will be those who don't believe my children are my own. There are hundreds of other details I don't know how to anticipate, because the women in my life have not been down this particular road. I love that my sisters have allowed me in on this part of their stories, but my body is always telling such different stories, and there doesn't seem to be any obvious place for them in the canon.

My perception of the certified picture of Womanhood and all the experiences, pains, and mile markers it entails doesn't just grow from personal conversations with friends and sisters. The wild world of social media has done amazing work to bring women together, and thanks to algorithms and momentum, it also manages to highlight universal experiences—or so we think.

Something as small and powerful as the unifying battle cry

#StopTellingWomenToSmile highlights a gap between my experience and that of many nondisabled women. Countless women are rightfully fed up with men who tell them to smile, but what does it mean that I can't think of a single time a man has ever told *me* to smile? I guess no one *expects* a disabled woman to smile? They see a wheelchair and anticipate drooping shoulders. A smile on a disabled woman is a feat, a wild victory, a triumph despite. When I smile, people stop to say, "Your smile is just beautiful." They applaud. They shed tiny ableist teardrops from the corners of their eyes, so moved by any glimmer of happiness they see from me. But my smile isn't some kind of tremendous accomplishment, some desperate, victorious climb to the top of a mountain. Sometimes it's just a video of a cat. Riding a robot vacuum. Wearing a shark costume.

I have one memory of being catcalled. One dusky evening on my way to a bar with a few friends, I pushed myself along the sidewalk in my turquoise dress with the lace collar and gray cowboy boots, and a drunk guy hollered at me from a block away on the main drag of my college town, "You're the hottest girl in a wheelchair I've ever seen!" I laughed as I kept rolling, but my friends were indignant. "Did he really just say that?" (In retrospect, I'm not sure whether they were annoyed that he catcalled me in general or whether they were upset because he'd added the wheelchair caveat to his call. Could they be mad about both? We didn't unpack it.) But if I'm being real with you? In the secret corners of my heart, I treasured the validation that I too had been accosted with some form of sexual objectification in the street. Even if it had been shrouded in a disability caveat. (So much so that, *apparently*, I felt drawn to pick that very same dress for my first date with Micah. I mean, I'm just piecing this together for the first time, but did catcalling drunk guy help me make one of the most important clothing decisions of my life?! What do we do with that??) Honest to god, though, I can't tell you how often I've thought fondly of that weird, drunken shout-out on the street.

I feel guilty even typing out this secret, because I don't want some misogynist using it as justification for future catcalls. (Not that I imagine a large population of misogynists will ever pick up this book, let alone make it to this chapter. But still! Imagine the one! Dear sole misogynist reading this book: you do not have permission to use my secret memory as justification for hollering at anyone in the street.)

My experience just doesn't match up with those I so often see touted as the Experiences of Women. In fact, there's this weird way in which they can seem to sit head to head, occupying opposing force fields. When I move down a street or through a store or post something online, I'm not worried that men will sexually objectify me, because I'm used to my sexuality being automatically erased, ignored, and denied by default. Like *Parks and Rec*'s "Sewage Joe" expresses so beautifully as he shares his low-bar standards for a love interest: "She can't be in a wheelchair, no cane, no gray hair." Old people and mobility-aid users are Sewage Joe's only discards, bodies that can't tempt even his filthy palate. (Yes, there are those few who fetishize the paralyzed female body. I've talked to some and ignored a lot of them in my DMs. I've found this variety of fetishization to be wrapped up in a lot of shame and confusion, and, in my experience, it's almost always relegated to the shielded secrecy of anonymous online spaces.) Current social norms seem to put me in the same category as grandmas—definitely off-limits for fucking but available to boost your Good Person points whenever you offer to carry their groceries.

It's not that I've never been afraid of men. Once when I was hanging out with a guy at his house late at night, his vibe changed abruptly, and I realized I wouldn't be able to get out and down the front steps without his help—my mind started racing—*What will I do if he decides he doesn't want me to leave?* In grad school, I started carrying pepper spray in my purse after the attention from a guy in my program started to feel less flattering and more alarming. I know what it's like to be on alert around men, it's just that, generally, when I'm out and about in the world—making my way home after a late dinner or finding my car after a movie—my mind is wrapped up in other, pressing concerns. When I'm moving down a street alone at night, I'm usually thinking about whether or not there's an accessible path to the restaurant or my car. What will I do if I encounter stairs I can't get up? What if I get trapped somewhere? Do I have enough battery left in my phone to call someone for help? My brain is focused on keeping people from seeing me as helpless so they won't approach me from behind and grab my handlebars or try to grab a wheel from me when I'm putting my chair in my car. I've been catcalled on the street only once, but I've been stuck without a ramp or approached with unsolicited offers to help countless times. I can't bring myself to use an Uber when

I'm alone because it's too scary to have my wheelchair disassembled in a car with a stranger; the ease with which they could keep my mobility from me, the helplessness of not being able to run if I need to—I feel too vulnerable. I don't have nightmares about men following me home, but one of my most recurring dreams involves being separated from my wheelchair. I'm left trying to navigate the world on my hands and knees—straining and frantic. I always wake up from this dream in a gasping sweat.

I don't know whether you can tell, but I'm having a hard time trying to pinpoint this intersection between Disabled and Woman. I find myself worrying that these questions will be received as an attempt to quiet or poke holes in or take away from the powerful collection of women's stories already gathered. This is not what I'm trying to do. *Listen to women! Street harassment is real and shitty! Stop assuming women are here for your gratification!* I admire women and the work they're doing to lift each other up. (Also, do you notice that I'm still talking about women like I'm not one of them? What is this?)

Maybe the tender center of what I'm trying to express is this: there's something disorienting about being both a Woman and Disabled. Because I can rationally agree that I am technically a part of this big group "Women." My closest friends are almost all women. I shop in the women's section of clothing stores. I usually find myself instinctually identifying with the women characters in storylines. Something like 86 percent of my followers on Instagram are women. And yet, when I see women represented, when women have the microphone, when women talk about being women—my grip on my role as a card-carrying

Woman feels less secure. Like I realize I've been mingling at the wrong party all night (don't mind me—I'm just going to quietly back out of the room before anyone notices).

I can feel myself straining to fit into a constructed notion of what it actually means to be a woman—the *verified* version. Womanhood means enduring harassment, men staring at your boobs in doctors' offices and bars, getting hit on by your male boss or the group of guys ordering drinks at your table, working twice as hard to get that promotion. Womanhood means getting married and/or having babies, or making the decision not to get married and/or have babies, or having your relatives constantly asking when you're getting married and/or having babies.

So what does it mean if men stare at my wheelchair, rather than my boobs, in public? What does it mean if my biggest employment concerns are being hired at all, knowing how to disclose my body's needs, asking for accommodations, or sacrificing my health to stay in a job just because it gets me good health insurance? If the default assumption is that, of course, no one wants to marry a disabled girl? If the choice to have or not have babies is infinitely more complicated than simply deciding what I want? If no one dares to ask me when I'm having babies, because they assume I can't conceive or won't be able to parent or shouldn't reproduce? Where does my disabled body fit into this narrative about Women? I wonder, does my disability swallow my womanhood? When people look at me, is my disability so loud and alienating that my womanhood is unrecognizable? And, a much more pressing question, *Why does it matter?*

In January 2017, women gathered under the mantle of feminism in cities all over the world to protest the inauguration of the "pussy-grabbing" Donald Trump to the office of US president. Right now, these organized marches have been recorded as the largest single-day protest in US history. I attended the Kansas City chapter of this protest with a homemade T-shirt and sign that said "Women's Rights, Disability Rights, HUMAN RIGHTS." (Everything I wanted to say took at least three hundred words and didn't look great on a poster. The words "Rights," "Women," "Disability," and "HUMAN" were about as simple as I could get.) Micah and I and two friends walked to the march. He helped me navigate the curbs and grass. There was an accessible port-a-potty that I was both grateful for and loath to use. There were pink pussy hats, "I'm With Her" signs, "Super Callous Fascist Racist Extra Braggadocios" signs, and "Love Is Love, Black Lives Matter, Climate Change Is Real, Immigrants Make America Great, Women's Rights Are Human Rights" signs. I didn't see any other posters about disability or other women using mobility aids. (Only in retrospect do I consider how many disabled women protested from home simply because of limited access.)

I left the march feeling love for every human who showed up. I felt amazed by the strength and grit of women, the stunning resistance of women, the boisterous defiance of women.

I also felt embarrassed by my sign. Isn't that crushing? I felt silly for trying to force disability into a conversation where it clearly seemed not to belong.

I think the term we'd use for this is "internalized ableism"—

the act of adopting the very ideology, absorbing the precise disdain, practicing the same disregard that is already harming me. It strikes me as a rather clinical description for such an intimate wound.

✳ ✳ ✳

In the middle of writing this chapter and wrestling with the intersection of disability, womanhood, and feminism, I have dinner with two of my favorite women. Alyssa and Maren walked with me and Micah to that march in 2017, and last year they officiated at our wedding ceremony. Beautifully. In the most classy-ass jumpsuits. On this particular summer night, we sit around the table eating gooey nachos. We talk about Einstein's brain and the hive minds of Navy Seals, and after the second round of margaritas, Alyssa says, "How's the writing going?"

I immediately drop my forehead to the table and groan. "It's fiiiiiiiine."

"Oh, okay, *not* the right question." She laughs.

"I'm trying to come up with something worthwhile to say about being a disabled woman and feminism, and I have nothing! I mean, bleh. Who *cares*?"

They laugh, which is what I want, but they also don't agree, which surprises me. And, to make things very meta, I find myself surprised by my surprise. Did I really expect them to confirm that disabled women don't have a place in feminism? Maybe a deep dark part of me did.

"I'm just not interested in writing a chapter that says #DoBetter feminism!" I say.

"Okay, but think about this—think how important it is for white feminism to be dismantled," Maren says. "Feminism is *better* when it's challenged to be more inclusive."

It's easy to agree with her. A feminism that considers the injuries and oppressions of *only* white women ultimately punishes women as it continues to participate in racism. I can also see that when feminism equates womanhood with vaginas, it continues to fuel the harms of transphobia. When feminism expands its understanding of what it means to be a woman, it's made stronger, better, richer.

"But disability? I mean, feminism is already concerned with so many intersectionalities," I counter. I picture all the signs at the Women's March—signs with slogans representing every political identity and social issue—and try to imagine feminism attempting to squeeze in one more identity, one more set of concerns, one more hashtag onto the protest signs. I continue talking, but I keep my eyes clamped closed as I confess, "I feel stupid raising my hand and saying, *Could you include me too, please?*" I make my voice small and pathetic and pretend to raise my hand like I'm a tiny, timid mouse-person.

But mid-performance, eyes closed, I see my younger self, hanging on to the edge of the pool while the girls splash each other in the center. I see the little person who'd rather pretend she's asleep than try to have a conversation about boys with the prettiest girls in the cutest jammies. This feeling—the one that's begging me to shut up, stay quiet, disappear, withdraw, retreat—

has its roots tangled deep in me. It's the coping mechanism that says *not* getting an invitation is actually better. Because once you're invited? People can see you. And that means a minefield of triggers and risks. *Better to just stay out of it. To find your own pocket of peace. To party solo.*

It's like Maren senses it. "But you're not asking to be included on behalf of just yourself," she says. "Right? You've been given this platform to speak on behalf of so many people. This isn't just about *you*."

And in that tiny moment, I can see all of us—growing up across the planet, trying to figure out the world around us with these bodies of ours that don't quite fit. I see us as little kids getting overwhelmed at birthday parties, at the dinner table with families that don't quite get it, flipping through magazines on our beds scouring the pages for even one picture that looks a little like us, going to our first school dances and dancing alone in our rooms, making cautious dreams and staying up late at night trying to solve the impossible puzzle of independence, recklessly navigating our first experiences with love and sex and friendship because we haven't been given one goddamn road map. Suddenly, I do see it. I'm not raising my hand for *me*. There's a big, beautiful population of folks who want—who deserve—to be included, too, and raising my hand for *us* feels different. Suddenly, I feel validation and urgency behind this conversation.

But again, I stop short. I may be disabled, but I'm also an educated, white, straight, cis woman who grew up in a middle-class household, with way too much education for my own good and, at least for now, a full-time job with health benefits. To top off this privileged castle in the sky, even if I were to lose my job and home, I have family who would catch me. Of all the disabled folks living in this country—in the world—I have a relatively cushy gig. I'm swimming in privileges I can't even fathom. "I'm not sure," I hesitate. "I'm like one tiny person. What do I even know? What can I say about Disability?"

"You're not trying to be 'The Voice of Disability,'" Alyssa says, placing heavy air quotes around this make-believe title.

"Right. Of course. There's no such thing. No universal experience of disability," I say, sounding a bit too condescending for a conversation where I'm actually the one flailing.

"Right," Alyssa says. "But you have *a* voice, and you've been handed this microphone. What *do* you know? What can you point to? Who can you bring with you?"

✳ ✳ ✳

In 2006 Christopher Bell published an essay titled "Introducing White Disability Studies: A Modest Proposal." In it, he voiced a criticism that many had felt for some time, namely, that the academic field of disability studies was churning with white disabled folks in mind and did an abysmal job of engaging the intersection of race and ethnicity in the conversations being had. The essay was widely read, made a name for Bell, and unfortunately remained locked in the tower of academia. This conversation needs to be more than theoretical. In the same way that feminism is weakened when it fails to integrate disabled folks into its fold, disability work that concerns itself with only the most privileged bodies is missing the point.

I think of all the disabled folks I've met online, all of the faces and backgrounds and bodies and experiences and expressions and captions and comments and feelings and stories and *You too?* moments. These people are strong and funny and sharp and full. They're good storytellers and create fantastic memes. They have important and frivolous and entertaining things to say. And these vibrant, creative, ordinary people are vulnerable to a world that consistently ignores, denies, and punishes them for their differences. It might be easy for me to dismiss or diminish my own experience, but when I picture my whole community together, raising our hands, every age and gender, ethnicity and citizenship status, living situation and level of education, sexuality, skin color, and size, it's also much easier to raise my hand with them and ask that all of us be included.

Not only do I feel motivated to raise my hand, but it's easier to see *why* our inclusion is important. As I picture all of us together, I see it: disability that represents only people like me is missing the point, and feminism that considers only nondisabled bodies is a shortsighted feminism that eventually runs out for every woman claiming its protection. We need each other.

A couple of years ago I attended a panel discussion featuring the voices of young women who'd already garnered notable success in their fields. There was a chef, a lawyer, someone in marketing, and a woman with a job I didn't really understand. The moderator introduced the panel as a diverse group of women from different backgrounds, cultures, and ethnicities. The moderator took time to emphasize the importance of hearing different perspectives, and I was glad to see this sentiment backed by some amount of intentionality—the woman with the mysterious job and the moderator seemed to be the only white women with access to the microphone.

I listened to their stories about working in kitchens with bosses who hit on them and punished them when the flirtiness wasn't reciprocated. Stories about waitressing long hours to make it through law school. Stories about rushing to drop kids off at daycare before speeding to work each morning. As the discussion unfolded, I recognized that this conversation wouldn't intersect much with my own experience as a disabled woman. And that felt okay—this feeling happens, and not every conversation has to be for me.

But near the end of the discussion, a woman in the audience asked, "How do you manage work-life balance?" All of the women on the panel chuckled. No one wanted the microphone. Reluctantly one of them said, "I'm not really the best person to speak to this. I haven't taken a day off in eleven years." Everyone laughed and she passed the mic to another woman. Her response was similar. "Work kind of *is* my life," she said, almost apologetically. "There are times that aren't as busy, but it's not uncommon for me to work a sixty-hour week." A third woman was the first to offer a tip: "I find exercise is really important. Even if it means getting up at four in the morning to spend an hour at the gym before the rest of my family wakes up, it's worth it."

I sat in the audience, stunned that these were the only responses provided. *Really? Is that it? Let's all just giggle about the impossibility of having both a career and a body with limits?* Nearly two years later, I still think about that conversation. Each woman on that panel presented themselves as living in bodies with endless resources, and they were there to model success from that position. How many women listening had bodies that could replicate that model? How many can sustain that approach for another ten years?

We live in a world that rewards women who can push themselves beyond their maximum capacity, but not a single woman alive can maintain that push indefinitely. What perspective might disabled women breathe into this conversation? What collaborative reimagination might ignite if we offer the microphone to people who've been navigating a relentless, unsustainable work setup with bodies that don't/can't/won't/shouldn't oblige—what do you think?

I'm not proposing that every single feminist conversation has to be about or for or even include disabled women. I *am* saying that erasing disabled women from our vision of what it means to be a woman limits *all* of us. And not in some abstract, theoretical way. Literally and truly—every single woman is subject to the demands, uncertainties, and limitations of her body—a body that strains under the forces of gravity and time, that wrinkles and breaks, swells and sags, accumulates pain and injury. Many of our bodies are literally torn by giving birth, transformed into food through lactation, and subject to the roller-coaster unpredictability of menstruation, menopause, and hormone therapy. The most consistent, most universal, most shared experience in having a body is that they all change, and if you live long enough, they all start to slow, forget, fracture, ignore orders, and revolt. When we pretend disability is not a part of womanhood—when we keep the two separate and distinct—we're all left less equipped, less adaptable for the inevitable challenges of life.

Honestly, I get it. It's not hard to see how the chasm between womanhood and disability formed. In our not-so-distant past, the "physical frailties" of women (which, yes, included monthly cycles, because, BLOOD!) were used as evidence that they shouldn't be educated, shouldn't work, shouldn't leave the house, shouldn't travel alone, blah, blah, blah. (Side note: Did you know that when public restrooms were first created, they existed only for men? Because, why would a woman ever be in public long enough to need a toilet out in the wild? TRUE STORY.) In order to assert that we *do* deserve education and work and the right to *exist in public*, women have felt the need to claim their strength and hide any perceived weaknesses. Because, in a very real way, they could be used as evidence to send us home. This has to be felt even more intensely from women who intersect with additional marginalized identities, women who don't need one more reason to be excluded, dismissed, or rejected. I also wonder what we've lost in our struggle to minimize these so-called weaknesses and prove we can fight just as hard. Can we be both gentle and strong? Fragile and resilient?

As we ignore or minimize our vulnerabilities, our most tender parts, our inherently human physical limitations, I wonder—are we just reinforcing the rules patriarchy wrote: *a body that doesn't have needs = ideal, valuable, worthy. A body that has needs = discard pile.* Not only are these rules utter bull-a-shit, but they're boring. What else is out there that we can't see beyond the towering fence of rougher-tougher-stronger patriarchy? What happens when we acknowledge the fact that all of our bodies need help, intervention, and support? And why not invite the experts on the front lines of adaptability and access to that conversation?

Not every feminist icon has to be disabled, but I wonder what we might lose when we look up to only the strongest, fiercest, youngest, and fittest—the ones who don't seem to age in any meaningful way beyond collecting a few graceful wrinkles and rocking white hair. What nuances and insights are we missing by our selectivity? Remember how the world flipped out when Selma Blair touted her cane on the red carpet at the *Vanity Fair* Oscar party? That image of her holding her cane in her billowy silky dress seemed to explode our brains. It showcased the tangled relationship between weakness and strength. It represented so much grace and poise and beauty, precisely in the moment she publicly embodied her diagnosis of multiple sclerosis.

What happens to womanhood when we always idealize the most able, the most "successful," the most independent? Just this morning, I was blasting Kesha's "Woman"—and I sang along, because I *am* a motherfucking woman, baby, and I *don't* need a man holding me too tight. So many feminist anthems (especially, as it turns out, the ones that I love belting out at the top of my lungs) honor independence as the highest form of female empowerment—buying lots of stuff with your own money, paying your own bills, not needing a man for anything. It feels really good to scream along.

In these cathartic moments, I channel the newly divorced Rebekah. Growing up, I never imagined I'd be able to pay my own bills. When I moved into my first apartment on my own, I'd been given complete access to a fully fueled rocket ship—the universe was mine. It didn't matter that the apartment was subsidized or that food stamps paid for my groceries or that my monthly checks were from the Social Security Administration. The fact that I was legally able to divorce my husband—against his will—was nothing less than an unquantifiable gift that existed only because women before me had fought *hard* to make it possible. Our independence is not something to gloss over. The freedom to vote, to own property, to divorce our spouses, to choose what happens to our bodies—these are game-changers.

And also. When I think a bit more about these kinds of lyrics, I can't help but think of Micah. My mind flashes to the recent, still-dark mornings I clung to Micah's shoulders as he helped me stand, slowly and painfully. I think of Micah taking off work and flying with me to a speaking gig so he can help me navigate the airports and stretch my spasming legs before bed and first thing in the morning. This year my body has deteriorated rapidly, and I've been leaning heavily on this man. I might even say I've become some kind of *dependent* on him, just as he was dependent on me when he broke his femur a couple of years ago. It doesn't feel stifling or limiting or disempowering (like the claustrophobia I felt in my first marriage). It feels sturdy. I still love these anthems—and so does Micah, by the way—and

I don't plan on taking songs like this off my playlists. They do a wonderful job of telling one important part of the story. But I also wonder: Do we lose something when we worship independence and villainize dependence? I get why freedom is everything, but do we miss out on interdependence when we cling so tightly to autonomy? I wonder, what could disabled women add to our conversations about the possibility of being an empowered independent/dependent woman?

Disabled women are a part of this, and while the shape of our stories can look different, we are also injured powerfully by patriarchy. In fact, some of the conversations most fundamental to feminism—violence against women, reproductive rights, equal pay—are left recklessly incomplete when we exclude the voices of disabled women. How can we fully dismantle patriarchy unless we've taken care to examine the range of wreckage left in its wake?

We can't have a complete conversation about violence against women without including the experiences of disabled women. The National Coalition Against Domestic Violence reports that disabled women are three times more likely to be sexually assaulted than their nondisabled peers and estimates that 80 percent of women with disabilities have survived sexual assault. Many disabled women have cognitive and/or communication impairments that abusers recognize as reasons these women are less likely to report abuse or be believed. Disabled women are also often put in a position of intimate reliance on their caregivers or their primary partners to help them go to the bathroom, bathe, get dressed, eat, and so on; if they report abuse, they risk losing care or being institutionalized. The 80 percent is not just made up of women who have difficulty communicating or are dependent on caregivers, however. Many articulate disabled women who don't rely on caregivers are part of this statistic, too. Like me. Maybe you and your friends, too. There are many tangled ways that disability adds to the already high risk of sexual assault that women face.

We can't talk about reproductive health or freedom without talking about the stigma surrounding disability and sexuality or the lack of education that disabled women experience when it comes to conversations about consent, pleasure, or contraceptives. Over the course of our history, disabled women have been forced and coerced into sterilization, pressured to have abortions, barred access to fertility treatments, and criticized for reproducing.

When we talk about "equal pay" for men and women, how do we ignore the unemployment rates for women with disabilities? It is actually and truly legal to pay disabled employees as little as pennies an hour for their labor. This has been practiced legally for decades, and there are companies doing this right now. How is this not part of our conversation about equal pay?

When you see it all together, gathered in a list, isn't it weird that these stories aren't a part of the discussion?

I keep thinking about the catcalling conversation in the fancy loft. I wonder, how else could that have unfolded? I've tried to imagine what would have happened if I *had* shared my stories—of being catcalled and secretly liking it, of being shouted at by men in parking lots who think I need them to help me get my chair into my car even as I do it with ease right before their eyes. Would my additions to the conversation have added complexity to our understanding of patriarchy? Would we have a better understanding of this force as we consider the effect it has on the women it targets *and* the women it ignores? Maybe the addition of these stories could invite a more collaborative exploration of the line between objectification and admiration or the relationship between patriarchy and ableism.

I don't know whether my stories would have moved us in this direction—I like to think so—but I do know the sole responsibility to push this conversation forward can't rest on the shoulders of those who've only recently been given a seat at the table. It's not enough to simply send the sparkly balloon invitation. Showing up to a space that has historically ignored, erased, or belittled you is scary and exhausting. But if the ones in charge of the party take a beat, listen to the newcomer, and make genuine space for difference, I believe everyone is given more—more room, more flexibility, more options. I mean, did every single girl at the swim party really want to be in the middle of the pool screaming and splashing? Maybe some of them longed to hang out on the side where the waves were calmer. Maybe some of them would have preferred not to get their hair wet at all. Maybe some of them wanted to go to sleep earlier, wanted to wear basketball shorts to bed, wanted to talk about cute girls instead of cute boys. There might be a little less for those who've grown used to having the whole table to themselves, but for the most part? I think including more voices means more for us all.

As feminism creates more space—as it evolves, expands, and grows in richness—I think it's becoming less a conversation about men and women and more a force to disrupt the crustiest, most established power structures. This stronger feminism asks who has power and who doesn't, where does that power come from, how do we disrupt the great disparity between the powerful and powerless, and what are alternate ways to access power while caring for each other? I think we sometimes make claims about the experiences of "all women," because we live in a world that is so often dismissive of those on the margins of established power. These stories should be heard and amplified. But I also think there are many more stories to add to the collection we have started. Nuance is harder to rally around or shout from a megaphone, but it's also sturdier and more sustainable. When we shout *"Ask any woman!"* I think we should. Ask. Listen. Adapt. Expand. It feels risky, I know. But so do swim parties.

1

THE COMPLICATIONS
OF KINDNESS

I am a magnet for kindness. Like the center of a black hole, my body attracts every good deed from across the expanse of the universe to the foot of my wheelchair. I move through parking lots and malls, farmers' markets and airports, bookstores and buffets, and people scramble to my aid. They open doors and reach out their arms to help, they offer prayers, grab my handlebars for a push, watch over me, and hold out wads of cash.

Okay, so not every single person who comes within my orbit suddenly sprints to my service. There are plenty of people who don't seem to notice me, and some people who are actually repelled by my magnet. They look down, pull their bag or their child closer to them, draw their legs up to their chest as I roll by. (Yeah, it doesn't feel *great*.) But it's the abundance of kindness that gets me all tangled. It's the fly that won't stop buzzing, won't hold still long enough for me to swat it, won't die.

It's harmless, really. What damage can a tiny fly do? But then why do I feel like tearing down the house every time I hear its familiar buzz? And here's the real nasty cherry on top of the fly: more than any other subject I write about, people do not like what I have to say about the complications of kindness. Because how could kindness be anything but good? What do I possibly want from the people if not kindness? And really, what kind of ungrateful hag must I be to complain about people trying to do nice things for me??? I've talked enough with folks to know— this conversation is uncomfortably disruptive.

✳ ✳ ✳

As a culture, Americans are pretty well convinced that disability is something they've figured out. In fact, this was a puzzle solved years ago. How could ableism exist when we've memorized the rules? Don't say the R-word; don't make fun; disability doesn't define anyone; just try to be helpful; and the rule that guides them all: *Be kind.* I've seen so many people perform these creeds in one form or another.

Like the folks who try to do me a favor by keeping me separate from this disabled body of mine: *All I see when I look at you is a beautiful woman. I don't even notice your wheelchair! I don't think of you as disabled.* It's meant as a kindness, but it feels like erasure. These words handpicked to soothe the wounds of disability are weapons themselves, reinforcing the deep-seated belief that beauty and value can't coexist with the deviations we all know I embody.

I think I understand how it happens: If you live in a community where disability is framed as tragic, sad, and inferior, then claiming not to see that so-called defect feels like a favor. We try to extract the disability from the person, because we think disability is ugly, and the rules tell us that this separation is nice. But do we attempt to extract thinness, Ivy League education, or wealth from a person? Of course not. We see these characteristics as inherently positive. Maybe individuals hold on to these features as part of their identity, maybe they don't, but as a culture, we don't take it upon ourselves to graciously inform people that we see past their fit bodies, fancy diplomas, and piles of cash. There is no urgency to ignore thinness, no discomfort in recognizing education, no knee-jerk desire to erase wealth. Deep within our cultural understanding of what it means to be a human with a body, we position disability below ability and at odds with health, beauty, wholeness, success, and happiness. But I don't need my paralyzed legs to be erased in order for me to be seen as able, healthy, beautiful, whole, successful, or happy.

Time and time again, people in my life and readers of my work become uncomfortable with, ruffled by, and hostile to the stories I share about sitting on the receiving end of "kindness." Maybe it's because so many of us claim "kindness" as one of the most important qualities a human can possess. Disrupting our understanding of kindness is a direct threat to our sense of self and understanding of the world around us. But as a veteran Kindness Magnet, I've found people's attempts to Be Kind can be anything from healing to humiliating, helpful to traumatic. It's complicated.

* * *

At least eight times a day, I yank and throw, pull and twist my wheelchair in and out of my affectionately beat-up 2007 Toyota Corolla. After more than a decade of practice, the entire ordeal takes about thirty seconds. In my head, I make these familiar transfers with grace and badass agility, but the reactions of kind strangers suggest otherwise.

On this particular day, I'm on my way into a coffee shop to grade papers. I'm assembling my chair like a wizard—I'm in the zone—when I hear a man yelling at me from across the parking lot. I tune him out. I'm used to pretending I don't hear people calling after me in parking lots. It's safe to assume he wants to help me, and I have decades of data to attest that he will not be able to make this routine even the slightest bit easier for me. I went through a phase in my early twenties when I used to let people try to help me. "Why not let them get that bright-smile boost that comes from playing the Good Samaritan?" I thought. But it usually took about six times as long to teach them the moves I could do so easily myself. My benevolence for my wanna-be caregivers didn't last very long.

So I'm in the middle of putting my chair together, and I can still hear the man yelling across the parking lot. Now I've got the body of the chair on the pavement by the driver's seat, and I'm reaching into the back seat for the first wheel. I'm swift and strong and capable. I'm sure it must look difficult for someone who's never seen it, but I don't falter. The wheel is firmly in my grip when my peripheral vision catches a glimpse of the man running toward me.

"Don't fall! Don't fall, don't fall!" he shouts. His hands are reaching toward me.

I pause and stare at him. I'm indignant and amused. Why does he think I'm falling?

"Oh, I'm fine!" I say. "See?" I pull the body of the chair upright and begin to slip the first wheel into position.

The man sways on his feet, seemingly torn. I might look fine, but surely I'm not. "Ehhhh," his face strains as he watches me. I quickly assemble the second wheel, flip the chair to face me, and stand up to transfer. "Ehhhh," he groans again, and, as if he can't restrain himself, he cries again, "Don't fall!"

I hop into my seat and grab my bags. I've lost my patience. I'm no longer trying to be pleasant. I've used my words and demonstrated through action: *I'm fine*. Why doesn't he see that? He rushes to open the door for me. I roll my eyes.

In my three decades of being disabled, the main messaging surrounding disabled people is that we're supposed to Be Nice to them (or maybe, its close cousin, Don't Be Mean). Regardless of our age, socioeconomic background, or education, we learn that disabled people need protection and assistance. If a disabled person is being made fun of, the Kind Person intervenes to say, "Stop that!" Or better yet, punches The Bully in the face and yells "Scram!" while The Bully scuttles away. The helpless disabled person becomes an opportunity for the Heroes and Villains to define themselves. If a Kind Person sees a disabled person struggling, they try to intervene. Offers their seat. Reaches out. (Especially if that disabled person isn't begging for money on the street or asking for more government funding to support their independence. Somehow these versions of help for the disabled tend to be categorized *very* differently from the cute little white woman in the parking lot of a Target putting her wheelchair into her car by herself.) One of my high school seniors articulated the feeling beautifully in one of our class discussions: "If I'm in public, and I ignore a disabled person who seems like they need help, I look like a dick. So I help, because I don't want people to think I'm a horrible person." From where I sit, he's not the only one who feels this way.

This is the power of the one-dimensional, deeply embedded, ableist script in our culture. Some bodies are Victims, others are Heroes. Some bodies need help, other bodies give help. We tell and retell these stories, and we feel really good when we do. Not only is this story common, it's cherished, revered, beloved. Like royal weddings or animals of different species cuddling, we cannot get enough of stories that involve kindness and disability. I know this because of the internet.

If you want to make a story go viral, find a disabled person and film yourself doing something really nice for them. (Okay, but don't *actually* do it!) This precise formula works, again and again. There is a whole genre of sensational internet stories just about cheerleaders and football stars asking disabled kids to the prom. Go ahead, Google it—you'll see: "High School Football Star Becomes Internet Sensation After Taking His Disabled

Best Friend to Prom and Leading Her in a Slow Dance" (the *Daily Mail*), "This Student with a Disability Got Asked to the Prom in the Sweetest Way" (*Buzzfeed*), and "'When Pigs Fly': Girl Asks Boy with Special Needs to Prom" (NBC4). Apparently, we love this shit.

In the summer of 2018, another story of kindness and disability exploded across the internet, appearing in sources from BBC News to the *New York Times*. In each retelling, we are brought into fifteen-year-old Clara Daly's experience. She was sitting on a flight when she heard the call, "Does anyone know sign language?" She learned that the flight included a deaf and blind passenger, Tim Cook, and the airline staff had no way to communicate with him. Daly had started learning sign language about a year before, and as she signed words into his palm, she became the conduit between Cook and the rest of his surroundings, telling him the time, getting him water when he was thirsty, and chatting with him during the boredom of their flight. There are four photos snapped from their encounter that day taken by a passenger who posted the story to her Facebook page. Her post was shared hundreds of thousands of times within the week. In three of the four photos, the camera focuses on Daly. She is the star of the shot, the face our eyes are drawn to. These images reappear in every news article. Daly's face is young and bright. Her blond hair and glowing cheeks look almost otherworldly under the light pouring in from the windows. Cook's face is obscured. We see the back of his head, the side of his beard on the edge of the cropped photo. He's presented as the side note, the shadow on the margins, the incidental object in the frame. The original viral Facebook post has since been taken down, but the author remembered the moment as a "beautiful reminder in this time of too much awfulness . . . that there are still good, good people who are willing to look out for each other." Daly herself expressed bewilderment over the viral status of the story.

In an interview with his local news station, Cook said he's used to isolation and thanked Daly for reaching out to him. This detail added a sprinkling of heartbreak to the story and remained unexamined. The title of the article wasn't "Deaf and Blind Man Sheds Light on Social Exclusion for Disabled Communities." The article didn't include a whiff of interest in solving the problem of disability stigma or social ostracism or even how to make airplanes more accessible for disabled folks. In fact, it seemed to hold tightly to the assumption that of course someone in this body would be isolated. More than anything, the actual events that unfolded were transformed into a gooey celebration of the forty-five minutes when one pretty girl talked with one disabled man on an airplane so that its readers could get the feeling of being wrapped in a hug. The whole world isn't fucked! Thank god.

I get it. The world is dark and scary, and we need more feel-good "news stories" to counteract the shitshow of current events. These news articles didn't attempt to fix the problem of ableism, but are they really so bad? I mean, isn't any form of reaching out, trying to help, being there for another person worth celebrating? The world is teeming with cruelty and hate—can't we pause over the bits of kindness we find?

But here's the problem: we have ignored the perspectives, stories, and voices of disabled people for so long that their *actual* needs, feelings, and experiences are hardly acknowledged, let alone understood, at all. Our default impulses draw us firmly and consistently into the perspective of "able-bodied helpers." We look through these people's eyes so regularly, are so eager to identify with them, so ready to celebrate their generosity that we forget to ask even one of the many questions hovering around the disabled recipients of "help." Like, how did this experience feel to you? Did you want anyone's help? Was it even helpful? What needs did you actually have in this moment that remained ignored or misunderstood? What could be put into place that would anticipate this need so that you aren't forced to be dependent on the kindness of a random stranger who may or may not be there next time? Did you know you were being filmed or photographed? Do you want those images shared? All over the entire internet? Did this moment make you feel like a spectacle? How many times have you been put in this position before?

These kinds of articles and social media posts refuse to look at the big picture. They don't unpack why there is such a social stigma around taking a disabled person to a school dance or why airlines will happily accept money from patrons like Tim Cook when they don't have any plans in place for accommodating them. In their attempts to celebrate something that looks like kindness, articles and posts like this only reinforce an old, punishing story that keeps disabled people on the outside, at a distance, and in the background.

* * *

I'm about seventeen, and I'm taking a school bus to St. Louis for a weekend youth group trip along with my boyfriend Sam. We're there as "leaders" for a group of middle schoolers, and twelve hours in, I'm already exhausted. We're scheduled to walk through some touristy St. Louis caves. They're clearly inaccessible, and I relish the thought of having an hour-long break.

As the group lines up near the entrance of the tour, I casually mention that I'll just meet them by the exit.

"Bek! I'll just carry you!" Sam says. Sam carries me a lot of places, and usually, it's welcome and easy. There are places my wheelchair can't go, and Sam's body becomes an extension of my own as we roam beyond the "handicapped accessible" bounds. I like that about us. But this time, I'm tired. Also, I don't give a shit about these caves.

"Sam, it's like a mile long in there," I say. "Don't be ridiculous."

"Aw, that's nothing!" he says, flexing his biceps like a cartoon superhero. He spends most of his days impersonating Mel Gibson in *Braveheart*. Carrying a girl through a cave would be very on-theme.

"No, really. I'm tapping out of this one," I say. "It'll be a nice break."

"Would you please just let me carry you?" Sam asks loudly. A few other people are listening now.

"I really don't want to," I mumble, trying to keep this a private conversation.

Sam kneels in front of me, looking up with his round kiwi-green eyes framed in dark lashes. "Please let me carry you," he says, quietly now.

"Aww," a few girls say in unison, close behind us.

I look from Sam to the cluster of girls watching us to the side. Why do I say yes? Who am I trying to please? What good do I think this will do?

We leave my wheelchair with one of the guides, and I wrap my arms around Sam's neck as he grabs my legs. We start the long hike through the dark, damp caves. One hundred feet in, I know I've made a giant mistake. My chest and cheek rest against Sam's quickly dampening back, and my arms and neck quickly start to ache. As we reach a tight corner, Sam bends down, and I see the bright white light of a camera flash behind us. I turn around to see one of the girls who gushed "Aww" a few minutes before, winding the film of her disposable camera. She continues to take pictures of Sam carrying me through the cave throughout the tour, more interested in the performance of hero and damsel than the caves themselves. If this had taken place today, would we have become another viral internet story? I can see it now: "Brave Boy Carries Disabled Girl Through Cave: There's Hope for Humankind After All!"

The trip in the cave feels like climbing across the circumference of the moon. With the thump of each step, I wonder whether my shoulders will pop out of their sockets. I feel like a piece of luggage, a deformity growing off Sam's back. When we finally make it to the other side of the cave, we have to wait a couple of minutes for my chair to arrive. Sam helps me prop myself against a wall as person after person congratulates him on carrying me so far.

"Dude, that was incredible," they say. "I can't believe you carried her that whole way."

Sam doesn't make a big deal out of it. Even so, I don't want him to touch me. When my chair finally arrives, I reach for it like my own mother.

✳ ✳ ✳

I'm twenty-four, recently divorced, and finding my way through the daily tasks of living on my own. I'm leaving the grocery store with a giant tote bag on my lap where I've arranged the tidiest pile of grapefruits, cartons of milk and yogurt, boxes of cereal and microwave popcorn. I'm proud of my grocery stacking abilities. I'm also well aware that the teetering tower of groceries looks precarious to onlookers and part of this ritual includes a series of breezy and bright "no thank yous" to the inevitable offers of help. I decline the help for several reasons, like I am truly doing just fine; bringing someone else into this dance would actually be more difficult than simply completing the routine task myself; and I love the feeling I get when I fill my giant tote, transfer it to my car, lug it into my apartment, and put each item into its designated corner in my cupboard. I know it looks like I don't, but really, I've got this.

On this particular evening, the light is fading and the air feels cool on my cheeks. I'm almost at my car when a man the age of my dad kindly offers to help me. "Oh, no thanks!" I say.

"I've got a whole system." I nod toward my passenger seat and swoosh my hands back and forth. *It's elaborate, and I don't want to teach you,* I'm trying to say.

He eyes me as if I've just claimed I'm about to jump clear over my car. "All right," he says, taking five steps back to lean against the car parked beside mine and crossing his arms over his belly. His eyes don't leave me or my groceries.

I start my routine: put the tote on the floor of the driver's side, transfer from my chair to the car, take the wheels off of my chair and throw them in the back seat, pull the frame of my wheelchair over my body and place it into the passenger seat, and finally, lift the giant tote of groceries over my body to nestle in the frame of my wheelchair for the drive home. A little involved, yes, but no more so than flossing your teeth or getting dressed in the morning or doing laundry—once you've done it twenty times, you don't even think about it.

I try to ignore the weight of the man's eyes on me, but I feel my hands start to shake. *Please just go away,* I beg him silently. My temples and upper lip feel damp. His presence feels like a challenge, a threat, a bet that I'm bluffing. I'm rushing and fumbling, but I've gotten through all of the steps except the last one. I'm trying to pull the grocery tote over my body, but it keeps getting stuck, and the more I pull, the more frantic I feel, the harder it is to breathe.

"Actually," I say, finally using my voice. "You're making me really uncomfortable. Could you please stop watching me?"

Without a word, he walks to the other side of the car and stands with his back to me, still no more than fifteen feet away.

So I can call out to him when I inevitably face the reality that I can't do this task on my own? I start pulling out each individual item from my tote and tossing it toward the passenger seat. I have to get out of here. The bag is made smaller, I yank it up and over, slam my door shut, and peel out of the parking lot. I make it through two lights before tears start pouring down my cheeks.

✳ ✳ ✳

I'm twenty-seven, living the life of a worn and weathered graduate student. I'm sitting alone in a busy coffee shop, earbuds tricking me into believing I'm invisible and alone despite the fact that every table around me is occupied. I'm in the throes of grading stacks of freshman English papers. As a girl nears my table, I keep working, hoping my busy fingers clicketing on the keys will drive her away, but I can see her in the periphery, standing within an arm's length, her smile bright and hopeful. I yank out one earbud and look up.

"Hi, I'm Lydia!" She beams.

"Hi, Lydia," I say. I smile, too. I'm hoping it's the kind that says, *You are intruding, but I am being patient with you.*

"What's your name?" Lydia asks.

Why would I tell you my name? I think. "Rebekah," I say.

"Hi, Rebekah. I was sitting at that table over there," she points to a spot across the room, "and I felt God put it on my heart to pray for you. Could I pray for your healing to be able to walk?"

Her smile is steady and sweet, and my head explodes with the word "No." *No. No. No, no, no, I do not want you to pray for my healing. As if my "happy ending" won't come until I move from place to place with legs instead of wheels?* Lydia can see the effects of childhood cancer on my incapacitated legs, but she can't see anything else.

She's taking a risk with me—reaching out into a world of strangers with an attempt at what I know she sees as kindness. But in a room full of all sorts of bodies, she has singled me out as the Defective, herself as the Pipeline to My Restoration. "Oh, no thanks," I say. "I don't think I'm comfortable with that." I'm feeling very proud of myself for saying no. No is a newer word in my vocabulary, and it gives me a surge of pride and guilt to use it now.

"I don't want to do anything that would make you feel uncomfortable," Lydia says. "Could I just pray a blessing over you?"

I pause. I reach for my no-word. But who says no to a blessing? I don't want to be the scowling woman in a wheelchair, raining on the parade of a smiling, optimistic do-gooder.

"Okay," I say.

Lydia puts a hand on my shoulder; my stomach reaches for my throat. Does she have to place her hands on me? In fact, why does she have to involve me at all? Couldn't she just as easily send a quick prayer from her seat? People are starting to look at us.

Lydia begins her prayer. "God, I want to pray a blessing over Rebekah this afternoon."

I stare at my hands in my lap, avoiding the glances at the table of med students to our left and an elderly couple to our right. What do they think of the spectacle unfolding in front of them?

"You love her more than all the stars in the sky and more than all the sands on the beaches," Lydia continues, her hand still resting on my stiff shoulder. "God, I pray that you would bring healing to Rebekah . . ."

Wait, healing? Healing, as in the prayer I said "no" to?

"Bring healing to Rebekah in whatever form she needs to be healed."

Very nice, I think. Such clever maneuvering. Maybe you'll get your way, and I'll rise from my chair and walk across the floor yet.

"Amen," she finishes.

"Thank you, Lydia. That was really kind of you," I say, loathing myself as I express gratitude for the very thing that has left me feeling so small.

Why can't I allow her to know how she has made me feel? Am I protecting her, or am I protecting myself? Lydia goes back to her table, and I stare at my reflection in the computer screen feeling empty. *Stop being dramatic,* I think. *A sweet girl prayed a blessing for you. It's like you're pouting about the kittens cuddling too hard.* And yet, my throat tightens, and my eyes well.

✳ ✳ ✳

These stories are just three of many sprinkled generously over my past thirty years. They capture a brand of self-serving kindness that seeks to fuel an ego, a kindness interested in claiming the heroic role in the story, a kindness that hardly notices the actual consequence of the "good deeds" being dispensed. Like holding up a metal rod in a lightning storm, I run a risk of being struck by this version of kindness whenever I leave my house.

This is the part of the essay when some readers start furrowing their brows. "So how am I supposed to be helpful? Are you telling me I can't open the door for a disabled person? I open the door for everyone! How do I know when someone does or doesn't want my help? What are the rules?" These inquiries remind me a bit of the kinds of questions that come up when we try to talk about sexual consent. Human beings are complicated, and communication can be nuanced. "No, please don't. This is making me uncomfortable," isn't always expressed directly through language. The point here is to pay attention to the human person in front of you. What signals are they giving you? What expression do you see on their face? Even if this isn't intuitive for you, pay attention to their eyes—are they avoiding your gaze or looking toward you like they want to engage? If you really can't tell, you can always ask, but if someone says, "No thank you," listen to them. You might get it wrong sometimes, but please don't let the discomfort of "messing up" make you throw up your hands and leave this conversation. Because this part right here? It's not really about you.

This deeply felt resistance I run into every time I suggest we complicate our understanding of kindness is so consistent I think it's worth interrogating. What does our attachment to this type of kindness give us? And why are we threatened by the proposition to loosen our grip on it? I have a guess based on my own firsthand experience of privilege.

When we're granted access to the world in a way that others aren't, we often feel guilty. Whether we recognize the source or not, there's a discomfort in watching another person struggle to navigate spaces that we move through with ease. We can alleviate some of that discomfort when we reach out a hand and pull someone along. *Phew! I'm not one of those regular privileged assholes. I care, dammit!* But our own discomfort is the driving force of that interaction, and when we're focused on alleviating our own uneasiness, we're not really looking into the face of the person whose hand we've grabbed. That feeling of discomfort is worth reflection—it's a red flag, signaling that something needs attention—but a gut reaction to discomfort can do more harm than good. Thoughtful reactions take time and reflection. What does the person in front of you actually need? Do you even know? Is this really an individual problem to solve in the moment? Or does this individual encounter reveal a structural change that needs to be made?

✳ ✳ ✳

I'm in the middle of running errands one afternoon, wearing my favorite steel-toe logging boots with red laces. I found them at a vintage warehouse shop. They're heavy and big and make me feel rugged and powerful. I pull up to the car repair shop and see a man watching me pull my chair out of my car and put it together on the pavement. This setup ends with my feeling small so regularly, my prickles spike before I even process the emotions. I feel the sweat pop out on my upper lip as I will myself to throw my chair together at turbo speed before he can read me as desperate and flailing. *I'm fine—I promise! Can you see how fast I'm moving? Can you tell how many times I've done this? Can you see how capable I am?*

And then I hear him. Such a simple, casual sentence. "Looks like you've got this," he says.

I look up. "Yes!" I say. "I really do."

* * *

When I finally found an affordable house to move into that was "accessible enough" after months and months of looking, I signed a lease as quickly as I could. The house had a couple of steps leading up to the front door, but this felt like a solvable problem. Surely someone out there could build a ramp for me. But I quickly realized this task was much more difficult to accomplish than I had imagined. I didn't really know where to start, so I called the Kansas City Housing Authority. After all, its expressed mission is to "develop, rehabilitate and manage decent, safe and sanitary quality affordable housing in a manner that promotes equal opportunity." I called and asked whether any programs were in place that could help me build a ramp for my house. They acted like I was a bit ridiculous for asking. I emailed a few individual builders, and they also acted like my request was rather absurd. Then, my brother found an organization called Hope Builders. Like good wizards with magic powers, this group of lovely humans came to my house, bought and brought all the supplies, and constructed an actual path of freedom into my house, all in one morning. Unlike putting my chair together, I needed their help with this. They'd identified a real and powerful need in our community and set to work addressing that need, practically and systematically.

* * *

I'm not here to tell anyone they shouldn't ever help a stranger in a parking lot or that a person has to start a nonprofit in order to be truly kind. But I do want to prompt a reexamination of when acts are, in fact, kind and helpful. In the ableist script that drives so many of our interactions, disabled people are either cast as helpless victims who need a hero's help to survive or the inspirational figures who inspire nondisabled characters to be grateful for their beautiful able-bodied lives. The reality is, of course, so much more complicated. Like anyone else, disabled people are both capable and in need of some help. Just like every other human, their competence and needs are unique. You have to pay attention to understand them. And it very well may be that the "kindest" thing you can do with that uncomfortable privilege you possess is to support an organization like Hope Builders.

So when I think about a kindness that does good to those on the receiving end, I'm not thinking about the person who hands me a napkin when they see me trying to reach the pile located on a high restaurant counter; instead, I'm thinking of the person who notices the napkins are out of reach for anyone who is shorter, uses a wheelchair, or can't stretch their arms and changes the location of the napkins. A kindness that brings about meaningful ease and access will lead to sustainable, systematic, empowering changes that make the world more accessible for more people. It sounds simple enough, doesn't it? Historically, though, the application of this form of kindness still gets easily tangled.

* * *

My best girl Bertie invites me to a fancy-pants fundraising gala for a charity organization that supports disabled kids. I pull a black dress from the back of my closet, straighten my hair, and put on a pair of pantyhose with one giant run down the back that I hide by remaining inconspicuously in my chair like a classy-ass lady. Turns out I haven't spent a lot of time circulating the fancy-pants gala scene, but I do my best to tidy up.

I'm nervous about attending this event, and not just because my usual wardrobe is mostly leggings and sweatshirts. With all of its dazzle and generosity, the premise of this organization—this event—rests squarely atop a fraught history. Disability and charity have long held hands in a confusing, often dysfunctional relationship that showcases how easily good intentions can slip into exploitation. Charles Dickens captured an early version of this dynamic with his pitiably frail and tirelessly chipper character Tiny Tim. Published in 1843, *A Christmas Carol* was written and read during a period when more and more people were being injured and impoverished by factory work, and Christian pastors were fervently preaching that their congregants should care for "the least of these." Enter Tiny Tim, the sweetest, sickest child you've ever met, complete with a little crutch and a heartbreaking cough. (Is his cough actually described in the book? I don't even remember! I just know I can't imagine Tiny Tim without a weak smile and an even weaker attempt to clear his lungs.) This little fellow serves as the ethical push Ebenezer Scrooge needs to complete his moral transformation. The only thing that can move Scrooge's cold, cold heart is the sight of Tiny Tim's tombstone, a death that could have been prevented by his very own bounty.

There is no doubt: this story is Scrooge's. Tiny Tim is here to inspire Scrooge's generosity, to transform him from a crusty miser to a joyful philanthropist. Yay! Our unlikely hero has discovered the secret to life! This story was written almost two hundred years ago, but it remains the default script we follow, and it hovers in the back of my mind as I get ready for the event, feeling cautious but hopeful. It's the twenty-first century, after all.

As soon as we move through the gold front doors to the bustle of the gala, I'm blown away by the glam and glitz. The opulent venue with shimmering, ornate ceilings and a red velvet–covered staircase, the twinkling chandeliers and staff circulating with delicate trays of bubbly beverages, the swishy dresses and dazzling smiles transport me. And it isn't just the lavish decor and costume. I'm quickly struck by the warmth, care, and passion I feel from the people behind the organization. We wander through a maze of round tables and make our way to our assigned seats where we find handwritten cards individually penned by the organizer of the event. She must've written hundreds of these cards! She visits our table radiating warmth and earnest goodness. Honestly, I think I can see sparkles in the air around her. She's the same onstage in front of swarms of people in their styled hair, suits, and pristine pantyhose. She describes the main goal of this organization, to raise funds to make Kansas City more accessible. This particular project aims to design an accessible park, because all of our kids deserve access to the outdoors. The vision she describes resonates to my core—let's make the world a more inclusive space for all of us. *Yes! Let's! Please!*

As I applaud wildly at my table, I feel at ease. I sip my fizzy gin and tonic, take bites out of every little treat on my plate (and Bertie's plate), and chat with the other poised and polished people at my table. While this organization still brands itself as a "charity," it seems to be setting its gaze at change that would actually empower the disabled community. Instead of simply setting us up to be dependent on a drip of gifts from our nondisabled benefactors, it seeks to reshape the landscape and pave the way for us to join the group through access. This feels good.

In the midst of my good vibes, Bertie and I decide we need more pasta. What's the point of dressing up fancy if it doesn't come with all the pasta you can eat? I push myself up the ramp along the edge of the room but start to lose steam about two-thirds of the way to the top. (It's steep. Also, I never work out. Also, gin and tonics.) Bertie gives me a boost, and we wander around the tables of food, eyeing each steaming tray of treats. As I roll along, winding through clusters of elegant socialites, a familiar feeling creeps over me. Moving through a crowded room of chatting people standing upright has never been my favorite. My body carries countless memories of similar scenes reaching way back to seventh grade when all the sweaty preteen bodies would pack tightly together before we were released for our first classes. It's a familiar feeling—being stuck, trapped, invisible, stared at, tripped over, talked over. But now I'm an adult wearing a black dress and pantyhose that appear to be fully intact. I can do this. I find the table with trays full of steamy noodles slathered in marinara sauce and hold out my plate for more, but still, there's an eerie feeling I can't shake. *What is this?* As I try to roll slowly down the ramp without the pasta plate sliding right off the incline on my lap, it dawns on me. I don't see any other visibly disabled adults here. Suddenly, I feel like I'm at a charity for zebras, and I'm the one who's escaped her cage and is roaming recklessly through the crowds of pretty party people.

As Bertie and I get back to our table, the lights are dimming and the program is just taking off. I'm soothed by the pictures of the park they're building. Universal design! Everybody wins! This is why we're here. They describe their mission, and I applaud. Then the gears shift to the "entertainment" part of the evening. They introduce the first performer with a video. He's a musician with a disabled sister. The film captures their closeness, their mutual affection. Then the musician brother comes onstage. He sings a few songs, we applaud, and I'm confused. *Why this musician? Why the video with the disabled sister? Are we supporting the sister by supporting her brother? Does the sister give the brother credibility to sing at a charity event? Were there no disabled singers available to perform at this gig? What is happening?*

Then the dancers come onstage. A group of teenage girls in matching leotards and streamer skirts prance onto the stage, each pushing a girl in a wheelchair. My entire body tenses. I sense a quiet, cold uneasiness move through the people sitting around me, and I wonder where their discomfort comes from. I imagine it isn't the same as mine. As I sit at my table, the only visibly disabled adult in the room, I'm thinking of my seven-year-old self, learning to swivel and spin in my first wheelchair. It was hot pink, and I loved the way it glided and spun, responding to the slightest pressure of my hands. I turned up Amy Grant on the radio and danced with my whole body and chair. I pieced together my own wheelchair dance routine with wheelies and backward zigzags. I imagined starting my own wheelchair dance classes. I loved to dance, and I danced hard, until my seven-year-old dreams were choked by the shame I learned to feel for my own body and the weird way it moved. *That's not dancing!*

I can barely breathe as I watch the girls onstage. The walking girls push the seated girls to the front, then begin the dance routine behind them. They move their arms and legs to the music, jumping and swaying, spinning and cascading in sync, while the girls in wheelchairs sit, fixed and planted at the front, some of them smiling, one of them waving her arms. In the middle of the performance, the dancers begin to push the girls in their wheelchairs around the stage. What is the purpose of this part of the performance? Is it for the benefit of the audience? Or the girls in their wheelchairs? Is this fun for them? I wonder, have these girls in their wheelchairs made up their own dances at home? Why can't we see those? There's a lot I don't understand about the scene unfolding on the stage, but one thing is clear: the girls on their legs are framed as the dancers, and the girls in their wheelchairs are used as props.

I don't know whether the girls in their wheelchairs enjoy their part in this performance. At least one of them seems to be having a great time. I do know that similar childhood rituals left their scars on me, even though I lacked the language to express the harm at the time. Sitting in the audience, watching this awkward dance, I'm now thinking of my nine-year-old self. Still with my hot-pink wheelchair, I sat with my mom on the stages of churches in front of audiences. I knew I was there to testify to God's unending goodness. I didn't quite know the meaning behind the words I was saying, but I knew a story was unfolding behind me that was much bigger than me. Just like the girls sitting at the front of the stage while the real dancers pranced behind them, I had been the smiling child-prop in performances, too.

After the dance number, the auction begins. This is the reason all the fancy people have gathered. This is my first real-life auction, and I'm enthralled by the hypnotic rhythm of the auctioneer's chatter. He's drawing out money from all the leather wallets and jeweled clutches like a human magnet, and the giant tally of funds accumulating slowly grows on the projected display behind him. As the evening goes on and donations thin, they start to bring some of the girls in wheelchairs back out onto the stage. They're young—no older than ten or eleven? One by one, each girl talks about how excited she is for the inclusive parks. One of the hosts, a man in a tuxedo, bends down with his microphone to ask one of the girls whether she has anything to say to the fancy people. "Please give us money!" she shouts. The room rumbles with sophisticated chuckles.

As I drive home that night, I feel gross. I want to celebrate the accessible parks, purely and simply. I don't want to be the crank, endlessly making a fuss over the problematic shortcomings of people just trying to make the world better. Why can't I just feel good about all the money they raised and move on? I genuinely believe the organization wants to make the world more inclusive for disabled folks. I also think they illustrate just how deep the roots of ableism run. Putting disabled people in the position of beggars is an old, punishing narrative, and while it's been known to prompt the feelings that lead to donations, it also perpetuates the ableism this organization strives to combat. It keeps disabled people in the position of helpless, small, and Other. We dismantle ableism and create inclusion when we flip that script—when we demonstrate that disability is a blurry, shifting category that prompts more care and flexibility and access for every human body. Even so and at the very same time, it's hard to hold on to the big, unwieldy picture when there are folks who need mobility aids and ramps and access—and they need them right now. The big picture asks for changes that take ages to accomplish, and we rarely have the luxury of waiting.

Days later, I still can't shake the feeling. I write a draft of an email to the woman running the organization, but in the end, I don't think I even consider sending it. I can't bear to criticize that lovely, well-intentioned woman.

* * *

After the man yelled "Don't fall! Don't fall!" across the parking lot, I got a cup of coffee and pulled up to a table with yet another stack of student papers to grade. I stared blankly out of the window, my mind running loops of complaints about all those ableists making assumptions and making me feel small. When I finally snapped out of my reverie, I realized I was running late to meet my friend Joe for a movie. He would be meeting me at my house in a few minutes. I rushed to my car, whipped the chair apart, and drove home at illegal speeds.

When I saw him waiting for me in my driveway, I rushed into apologies for being late. "Good grief, I'm so sorry, Joe! Why am I always late everywhere all the time? Before we leave, I just have to grab something from the house real quick, oh, but Joe, you wouldn't believe the man in the parking lot today!" As I plunged toward the house, I recounted, with the animated speed provided by caffeine and adrenaline, the man's obtuse assumptions about my capabilities. "He just kept yelling, 'Don't fall, don't fall!' at me!" I said. The sun was bright, the air was warm, and I felt strong and powerful as I recounted the man's absurdity in light of my obvious strength and agility. I arrived at the bottom of the ramp that led up to the back door of my house, and like an obnoxiously sunshiny cartoon character, I threw up my arms and shouted, "Isn't it beautiful today?!" My front wheels hit the edge of the ramp, and I felt my body flying through the air. Time slowed enough for me to form the thought, "Oh, you've got to be fucking kidding me," just as my knees hit the concrete.

I had fallen, hard. The worried man in the parking lot had just arrived two hours too early.

Joe and I giggled over the irony. I got back into my chair. We went to the movie.

This was not the first time I had fallen. Not by a long shot. There was the day in eighth grade when Bertie pushed me full speed across the grass as we hit a lump of dirt. I catapulted out of the chair, and Bertie froze as teachers rushed to the scene. The day I held my baby niece in my arms, feeling strong as I leaned against the wall just as my legs gave out and we both crumpled to the floor. She howled as I passed her off to my sister and sped to a back room where I could cry alone. The first time I fell in front of Micah, leaping from my chair and dramatically, ungracefully smacking my butt against the stack of books piled next to the bed where I had intended to land. How many times had I fallen in the bathroom, my wet feet slipping just before I heard the thwack of my tailbone on the tiles? So, yeah. I fall a lot.

Several years ago, my friend Amanda and I were crossing the street when my front wheels hit a crack in the road and I flew out of my chair in the middle of the crosswalk. My knees hit the ground, and my brain burst into one hundred different thoughts, one of which was an impulse to immediately console Amanda. I'm so used to people panicking when my disabled body pushes itself to the spotlight. (*Don't fall! Don't fall!*) I was desperate to convince her that I was really okay.

Instead, it went like this: I scrambled back into my chair faster than I had fallen out of it, and Amanda took a beat. She didn't hover or shout, didn't seem anxious or dramatic. She just watched me settle back in my chair and then said, "You are a fucking badass." After a lifetime of using a wheelchair to get around, I'm used to being told I'm helpless, even when I know my strength. But Amanda recognized grit in a scene most people read as weak. She caught hold of my slippery dignity, protected it while I climbed up into my chair, and then handed it back, intact.

When I imagine the shape of kindness that actually feels like kindness, it necessarily includes the pieces of this moment with Amanda: dignity and an unwavering understanding that falling is not the worst thing that can happen to a person.

The goal is not to avoid falling or needing help. The goal is to be seen, asked, heard, believed, valued as we are, allowed to exist in these exact bodies, invited to the party, and encouraged to dance however we want to.

I still think about that gala. How do we win at a game where our status as "loser" is already written into the rules? How do we represent disability with nuance over the roar of viral "promposals" from the captain of the football team to the disabled girl in his class? These are the stories people want to hear about disability, and yet they're the stories where disability exists only as the shadow hovering on the edge of the frame, here to make the nondisabled helper at the center of the story look good and feel hopeful. But I think this is the very place where nondisabled people have the power to do the most good for everyone, disabled and not yet there. If you want to be genuinely, actively, real-deal "kind" to disabled people, invite disabled voices into your organizations, businesses, and programs. Allow disabled people to perform in more roles than the grateful recipient of generous philanthropists. Recruit disabled engineers and dancers and office administrators and comedians and lawyers and speakers and teachers to participate in your world, and do your best to make that world accessible to them. And if we insist on using the "kindness" word to describe this kind of inclusion, we have to recognize that inclusive "kindness" isn't just a favor extended to disabled people; including disabled people is a kindness for all of us. Because listening to voices that are typically silenced brings to the table nuance, endurance, creativity, beauty, innovation, and power.

8

WHAT I MEAN WHEN I TALK ABOUT "ACCESSIBILITY"

The day my friend Joe proposed to my best friend Bertie, I felt a lot of things. I was happy they were happy. I was proud of myself for keeping the proposal a secret (Bertie's mom didn't think I could do it, and I did it, goddammit!), and I couldn't wait to help Bertie plan her wedding (although, she didn't actually need an ounce of help from me, having the best taste of any real-life human I know—really, you should have seen her wedding dresses—*plural*). And yet, among the giddy squeals and over-enthusiastic Pinterest pinning, there was also a pang of sadness. I knew this meant moving out of the house Bertie and I were sharing.

Four years before, I'd left my marriage to build a life on my own. I'd been living solo in a subsidized apartment, buying my own groceries, cleaning up my own messes, and, for good and bad, spending so much time alone. I finished my bachelor's and master's degrees and started my PhD program in that apartment. For the first time, I felt capable and in charge of my own story. So when Bertie said she needed a roommate, it felt like a dream coming true. Here I was building a life that I wanted to live in, and it was sturdy enough to expand and explore. I worried about being able to afford paying rent on a place that wasn't set aside for poor, disabled, and/or old folks, and I wasn't quite sure we could even find a place that was accessible, but I took a leap, because it felt like the universe was on my side.

We searched for a few tense months. I felt heavy waves of guilt for making Bertie's search so much harder—with any other roommate, she'd have infinitely more options. (Seriously, search for any kind of housing on any website. Then adjust your settings to include "accessible" housing—and *presto!*— watch all the options magically disappear.) But right before we were about to ditch the plan and set Bertie free to move on to an alternate plan that didn't include her disabled sidekick, we found a little two-bedroom house on Rainbow Boulevard. The house had a few stairs leading up to the back door and one more big step just inside. Bertie was confident that her engineer dad could build a handy ramp (which later proved to be a much more complicated project than either of us imagined—I mean, truly, a real-life puzzle—thank you, Bob!). We told the landlord we'd take it. It felt like a lucky find, but I also felt like we'd put in the time. It wasn't until later that I understood just how lucky we'd been.

The house was right across the street from a Chinese take-out restaurant and a vet hospital with a vibrant animal mural painted on the side of the building. Bertie found a bright orange vintage sofa on Craigslist, and we set to work filling the place with books and succulents. We threw themed parties and complained about our days over wine and popcorn. We drank lattes and ate noodles on the porch (but never sat on the porch swing, because my brother-in-law installed it with the caveat that it couldn't hold the weight of a real human, and we should never ever try to actually swing on it if we valued our lives). I made passive-aggressive comments about the dishes left in the sink, and Bertie started sleeping to the sound of two fans to cut out the noise of my cats getting restless at three in the morning. This was the single adult lady life I'd wanted but hadn't believed I could live. I saw myself as a pilot who'd guided her plane into the perfect landing.

And then Joe proposed, and he and Bertie decided they didn't want a long engagement, and before I'd even gotten used to seeing that giant ring on her hand, they were looking at houses together.

"What should we do with the orange couch?" she asked me. "I don't think we'll take it with us to our house."

I concentrated on painting my nails, trying not to cry. "Well, we can't just donate it for some boring person to buy!" I said, sounding like a sixteen-year-old version of myself appalled at my out-of-touch mother and her inability to understand what was at stake here. The orange couch was sacred!

As Bertie dove into wedding planning and picking out rugs

for her new house, I dipped my smallest toe into the shallowest pool of home hunting for myself. I was reluctant, a little pouty, and at times just plain sad. Every time I opened my laptop to test the waters, the sparse options dampened my already weak motivation. Again and again, I clamped the laptop closed, until suddenly, I noticed it was March and Bertie was moving out in May. My moping started to tangle into anxiety. It was time to get serious.

I pinpointed my parameters. It had to be affordable on a graduate-student budget (can we even call it a "budget" when the paychecks are that small?), and I had to be able to get in and out of it. If I could move around the space without enormous barriers, that would be cool. Not the *most* demanding parameters the viewers of HGTV have ever seen, I imagine.

I started asking around to my mom and my sisters, my closest friends and their boyfriends, my boyfriend and my dad. Have you heard of any places? Do you know anyone moving? Have you seen any "For Rent" signs? They'd send me Craigslist and Apartments.com listings and track down leads from friends of friends. Joe and Bertie spent a whole afternoon driving around town visiting places with me. I had a whole network of loving, smart people on the lookout. Something had to materialize soon.

We visited affordable apartments with dirty bathrooms and carpets, one accessible unit per building (that *might* be available in a month or two?), and no accessible parking. There was the unit that was advertised as accessible but actually had street parking on a steep hill and trash bins located across a street with no curb-cuts. After a few months of looking, there seemed to be three basic categories of housing:

1. Places that were affordable but inaccessible (with parking, laundry units, and bathrooms I couldn't access and a nice sprinkling of stairs)

2. Places designated for low-income, disabled people with waiting lists in the hundreds (I've had my name on three waiting lists for subsidized developments like this in Kansas City, and my name hasn't reached the top of any list in four years. One place actually sends me letters each year, asking whether I want to keep my name on the list, and I keep saying yes, because, by the time I actually make it to the top—in ten years? fifteen?—who even knows where I'll be or what I'll need)

3. Places that were brilliantly accessible (with sleek floors, wide doorways, and elevators) and spectacularly unaffordable

After several months of scouring the internet, my then-boyfriend Micah and I (we hadn't known each other for even a year yet) decided to drive up and down the streets of Kansas City (and all its sprawling pockets) looking for any space that might work. Maybe there'd be a magic unicorn building hiding behind a big tree? We hoped. That night we drove around, listening to

Vampire Weekend's new album and talking about my upcoming French exam. The hours passed as we made our way across the city, but we hadn't spotted one place to look into. Seemingly out of nowhere, Micah started crying. "How is it possible that this city doesn't have any place for you to live?"

"Oh, don't worry. It's okay! We'll find someplace!" I said, instinctually. I rubbed my hand in circles against his back, willing the weight of inaccessibility off his shoulders. But it was a burden I couldn't lift. What Micah had believed to be a series of annoying inconveniences revealed itself as a reality much gnarlier, more powerful, and consuming. This wasn't a pesky problem to bat away. It was a problem that defines and dictates.

As Bertie started to move her stuff out of our house and into her new home with Joe, I had to come to terms with the fact that despite the collaborative efforts of all my people, I still hadn't found a place to live. I secretly wished Micah would ask me to find a house with him. Our combined incomes would allow for more options. But even as I hoped for it, I felt gross for wanting the progress of our relationship to be determined by my housing situation. So, that spring, as I bought a bridesmaid dress for my best friend's wedding, I moved back in with my parents at the age of twenty-nine. This was simultaneously a great relief and a profound defeat.

On one hand, I was so grateful to have a place to go. This is not the case for many folks—a reality that felt closer, but still hardly fathomable to me. Had I not been caught by this net of support, there are other ways this could have gone. Disabled folks are often forced into homelessness, nursing homes, or subsidized housing far away from all that's familiar to them. They can feel like a burden staying with relatives or friends. Sometimes they stay in horrible relationships because they need shelter. I was keenly aware of this.

On the other hand, I was embarrassed and deflated to be moving back home at twenty-nine. I was burrowing into my childhood bed each night, staring relentlessly into the glow of late-night Craigslist searches. It didn't help that the only bathroom I could access in the house was in my parents' bedroom. I'd get home late in the evenings and sneak into their dark room, listening to my dad's snores and trying not to bang my chair into their antique dresser. Micah would come over to watch Netflix (in my childhood bed), and my mom would bring us a bowl of popcorn and a plate of apple slices. (Did you forget that I was almost thirty? Yeah, me neither.) The longer I lived there, the more ashamed I felt. I'd drive home from a day of teaching, pull into my parents' driveway, and feel about as capable of taking control of my own life as a tween.

✳ ✳ ✳

I spend a lot of time at the thrift store down the street, self-soothing by buying the weirdest mugs I can find and cheap, gold-sequin tops I'll probably only wear once. One day, I'm waiting in line for the single accessible dressing room with an older woman who walks with a shuffle. She sits on the lumpy

floral couch beside me, staring blankly toward the rack of tangled purses—prepared to wait. This isn't the first time we've
sat here together. In fact, I've come to expect the accessible
dressing room to be occupied by two friends who can't bear to
separate or someone with a full shopping cart of clothes. Five
inaccessible stalls sit empty beside us, their doors gaping open,
just in case we hadn't noticed the unused, and unusable, spaces.

It's not always obvious who needs the extra space or a place
to sit. The designated "accessible" signal features a wheelchair, but
that's not the only type of body with an extra layer of need. On
this occasion, though, as the older woman and I sit and wait, we
feel it: these two shoppers in the dressing room just want a bigger
room, and they want it all afternoon. We listen to them rum-
mage through clanking hangers, chitchatting casually as they put
on a full-fledged fashion show for each other. They sound a little
sleepy, like they've just had a big lunch, and they're ready for a nap.
"What do you think of this skirt?" one asks. I see her feet moving
below the door. She takes a few, slow steps in a circle. I can picture
her straining her neck to see the view from behind. The blue accessible symbol blares brightly on the side of the door facing me.

"I like it," the guy says, sounding bored.

"Are you sure?" More spinning.

"Here, try it on with this shirt."

She drops one shirt into the pile of clothes I've been watching accumulate on the floor. There's a lot of denim.

Twenty minutes later, on a ragey whim, I knock on the door.
There's no response. I hear his voice whisper, "Are they knocking
on our door?"

I chime in, "Hey! Yeah! Just wondering if y'all have an ETA. There are two people waiting out here for the accessible dressing room." I keep my voice light and bright. I'm so careful not to put them on the defensive.

After a confused pause, the same voice says, "We've got one outfit left to try on."

The woman on the couch glances over at me—the first time since we've been sitting side by side—and whispers, "Nice!" She gives me a thumbs-up and a wink.

I feel proud of my small intervention. Until I realize it doesn't matter. The pair proceeds along with the same rhythm, seemingly unmoved by my friendly prompt. When they exit five minutes later, the guy looks over and past us. No words. No eye contact. He has a few clothes draped over his forearm, and he takes long, slow steps. The woman glances at us and apologizes quickly and quietly. She keeps her eyes to the floor as they walk off. Were they embarrassed? Annoyed? Indifferent? Did they talk about this moments later? Will they even remember it happened by the time they get to their car?

Now that I have the space, I rush to try on my handful of dresses. I can picture the woman still sitting on the lumpy floral couch. How long has she waited for this accessible space now? Thirty minutes? Thirty-five? My anxiety starts to simmer. I think I should've let her go first. I yank dresses over my head, not taking the time to pull the skirt over my bum before moving on to the next thing. The space is big enough for my whole chair, even with a bench where someone like the woman waiting outside the door might sit. This is better than a lot of "accessible" dressing rooms I've seen, which are often either crowded with storage or just big enough for my chair to fit inside, but not big enough for me to put my feet on the ground to pull up a skirt. There aren't any handrails in this dressing room, though, so I put my weight on the hook used for hangers, trying not to lean too heavily on it. I've broken these kinds of hooks before, using them as a stand-in for handrails when they're designed to hold the weight of only a few sweaters and dresses. It's hard to be careful when I'm rushing, and I feel it strain under my grip. I gasp and let go, falling back in my chair. Time to wrap this up.

I fly out of the room, shouting "Your turn!" before I'm through the door. The older woman shuffles in with her tiny bundle of clothes to try on. Nothing about this half hour we've shared together seems to ruffle her too much. As if this is exactly what she expects from the world. My heart surges. *You deserve better!* I think. *You deserve consideration, respect, the space to try on clothes without waiting half an hour for punkass shoppers to finally tire themselves out! Your aging body is a wonder. A miracle of defiance and survival. There should be a red carpet unfurling two feet in front of your every step!* My neck and cheeks are hot. My resentment doubles, enough for her and me. (Why is it so much easier to feel indignant for someone else?)

But if this experience seems routine to her, I have to admit that it is for me, too. I'm used to waiting three times as long or not having a place at all. I'm trained to claim as little space as possible, cautiously and apologetically, to avoid irritating people, not just because I hate when anyone is mad at me, but mad people also tend to be less accommodating. It's an overly rehearsed scene with lines I can perform in my sleep.

So our experiences overlap, but we seem to receive them differently, and I think I can piece together part of the reason why. As someone who grew up after the passage of the 1990 Americans with Disabilities Act, I have a fundamentally different perspective than most disabled people born much before me. People like my friend Ruby and her husband Bruce, both wheelchair users and rebellious disability activists and advocates, who have been demanding access to participate in their communities since the 1960s and 1970s. Relentless efforts like theirs labored the ADA into existence. I understand that it's because of the ones who came before me that I'm able to occupy as much space as I do. I want to thank them for every ramp, every lift, every accessible dressing room.

George H. W. Bush signed the ADA into law in 1990, just a few months after around one thousand disability activists showed up at the eighty-three steps in front of our nation's Capitol, a building that many of them could not enter without elaborate assistance. After hours of speeches and protesting, sixty activists took to the stairs, many of them dragging their bodies up each step, literally demonstrating the spectacle—the social and physical discomfort—required to make it inside the political hub of the United States. Did you learn about this part of our history in school? Neither did I. The country hardly noticed the protests or the signing of the act. It was not a sexy news story. Unless you were one of the activists who had taken to the Capitol steps in an effort to be seen, acknowledged, maybe even valued, or one of the builders under new, largely misunderstood parameters, people didn't pay much attention.

From where I sit in a post-ADA world, it's easy for me to detect the overwhelming disregard, misunderstanding, sometimes disdain, and ubiquitous oblivion surrounding the original vision behind this piece of legislation. My students rarely know what I'm talking about when I mention the ADA, and I've had medical professionals cock their heads in confusion—*What is this A-DEE-A thing you speak of?* It's recorded as law, but it wasn't a law voted into reality by The People. It was handed to them from on high, and without great marketing. At best, the law quietly insisted that disabled people were humans, too. At worst, it embittered the public against those grabby, demanding cripples. Bit by bit, architecture began to change, not necessarily because our mainstream culture wanted to include a group of people they saw as possessing anything unique and valuable, but because the law demanded it. Owners of public buildings were required to make accommodations that many viewed as frivolous, inconvenient, and much too expensive for the payoff.

In fact, Americans understood and valued the ADA so little that about twenty-five years after it was signed into law, representatives from Texas and California dreamed up HR 620, the "ADA Education and Reform Act of 2017," which sought to dismantle the bit of relief that the ADA offers by placing even more burden on disabled people to defend themselves and demand their rights to access. In February 2018, the bill passed in the House with

225 yeas and 192 nays. It wasn't brought to a vote in the Senate, largely due to the efforts of Tammy Duckworth, a disabled senator from Illinois, who led a Democratic pledge to block the legislation. The bill died before going to a vote thanks to one disabled woman speaking up for a community that is still so often silenced. I wonder when or if access will become a concern in the forefront of everyone's minds, not just the ones who don't have it.

The revisions being made (or requested) for disabled bodies are often seen as extra. But this perspective holds up only because ableism is built on self-delusion; we tell ourselves the story that accessibility is a concern for only the disabled body, conveniently ignoring every form of access that has been carefully, painstakingly breathed into existence to make life easier for nondisabled bodies.

Let's take a giant step back and look at this together, like aliens watching from another planet. Someone, somewhere, at some point in time invented stairs, right? And since then, we've continued to build stairs, because they're easier for bipeds than scaling walls or climbing rope ladders. We have cars and bikes, because we want to travel faster and farther than our limited bodies can manage on their own. Parking lots and roads were made because people wanted easier pathways for driving their vehicles. Without intervention on behalf of the human body we'd all be sleeping on the grass, drinking lake water from our cupped hands, living every day of sweltering summer heat and frigid winter snows in all our radiant nakedness. Mattresses, cups, and clothes exist because the human body has limits, and tools make surviving this planet a bit easier. Literally everything that's been built—every signpost and path out in nature, every building and bus in our cities, every doorknob and chair in your house—was made to accommodate somebody. We stop refining or expanding our accommodations only when we're satisfied that those we want at the party can get there.

But our accommodations go only so far, because for a good, long while, we've cared to include only a specific kind of body/mind in our communities. Conversations about access for disabled folks didn't even start in the United States until disabled World War II vets demanded job training and rehabilitation after their return. It wasn't until 1973 that we passed the first piece of legislation that said, *Yes, you too. We think disabled folks deserve to exist here, too.* Accommodations for disabled people aren't "special." At least, not any more special than the world of accommodations already surrounding us. It's just that, typically, those who already have access haven't had to think about who is still waiting to be included.

And yet, when we consider disabled bodies as a vital part of the larger group, all of us benefit. When curb-cuts were originally designed, the idea was to create accommodations for wheelchair users. Prompted by the smallest whiff of creative innovation, curb-cuts were imagined into being as alternate options for interacting with our physical spaces, and suddenly, wheelchair users were granted access to more of their own neighborhoods and public spaces. But something else happened, too. Parents pushing strollers found trips around the block a bit easier. And so did people on bikes and scooters, people rolling luggage, vendors with food carts, people in pain who needed to take smaller, more gradual steps. Closed-captioning provides those with hearing impairments a way to access the stories and news delivered through their screens, but it also allows everyone the chance to connect with videos, even when they need to turn the sound off on their device or can't understand a mumbler. The medical model of disability—the default setting that sees individual broken bodies in need of individual solutions—misses so many opportunities to imagine a more flexible, accessible, inclusive, inviting world for all of us. What innovations might be made to medicine if disabled bodies were seen as conduits for innovation? What possibilities for play are we missing on our playgrounds? What practices might we adopt in our educational systems to facilitate more flexible, more meaningful learning for more students? What ways of being in the world might surface if we were able to lift the stigma clinging so tightly to the disabled body? What would happen if we decided disabled bodies were worth including?

When I say "included," I don't mean just the dressing room designated as the "accessible" space or the handful of first-floor apartments across an entire city designated as the "accessible" units. Access is more than the moment one disabled body bumps into one accommodating object. Access is a way of life, a relationship between you and the world around you; it's a posture, a belief about your role in your community, about the value of your presence. There's a fundamental difference between the experience of the person who wakes up taking for granted that they will, of course, have access, and the one who wakes up and wonders whether they'll have access, how they'll find or fight for their access, what they'll do when they don't have access.

How do I make this real? Even though I know in my head that I have every right to be here, I've also been shaped—from the ground up—by a lifetime of inaccessibility, and because of this, there's still so much I don't know about myself.

For instance, I don't know if I'm a "bar" person. It's hard to tell. When I roll into a bar, the bartender doesn't see me—or maybe just the very top of my head, if they're looking for it. If I'm able to shout loud enough, wave my arms wildly enough to be seen and heard to order a drink, I turn around to a room full of people standing, talking a good two or three feet above my head. When I speak, they don't hear me. So I shout over the talking and the music, and they lean down, angling their ears to my mouth. They nod and pretend they got all of that.

I don't know if I like trying new things. I mean, every part of me wants to say, *I do! I love new things! Let's try more!* But then a friend invites me to her birthday party at a new pizza joint, and I spend two hours Google Earthing the spot, squinting my eyes across grainy images, scouring the restaurant's crappy website for info on parking to assess whether or not I'll be able to get in the restaurant, and when I can't figure it out, and my breathing gets short, I send a quick text to say, "I'm not feeling well—so sorry I won't be able to make it!" Then I spend the rest of the night hitting "next episode" on *Criminal Minds* and listening to my brain repeat, "What is *wrong* with you?"

I don't know if I care enough about my students. Last spring, I got invite after invite to attend my seniors' graduation parties. My heart sang, *Yes! Let's celebrate!* Then I starred all of the invites in my email and waited weeks to respond. In that time, my brain flipped through imaginary visions of each venue and home, all of the emails and conversations I'd have to have to plan how I'd get through front doors or onto patios. I thought about dads lifting me and my chair up flights of stairs or aunts moving end tables or stacks of books or house plants out of my way—all of the quick damage control my body would inspire. My anxiety mounted. I sent out apology emails to each one, saying I was so sorry I wouldn't be able to make it, never giving the real reason why. I'm not sure how much my absence was noticed, but I felt weak and small, frustrated and disappointed.

I don't know if I fit in. I feel like an outsider with most people. How much is based on the fact that, as we navigate an environment together—the restaurant or park or bumpy sidewalk—a good quarter of my brain power is put into carrying that cup of coffee without spilling it or keeping my eye on the accessible route? How much of it comes back to the fact that I'm always taking a different path to get to meetings and gatherings?—I'm on the elevator while everyone else climbs the stairs; I'm flying down the ramp while others take the direct route; I'm driving to the conference in my accessible car while they take the train together. Some of this could be remedied if I'd just say, "Hey, someone ride in my car!" And sometimes folks take the elevator with me. But I'm already feeling like the weirdo. Like a middle schooler who prefers to remain under the radar—I'll just stay invisible over here, thanks! I don't always have it in me to ask people to join me on my roundabout path.

These moments add up—so rapidly and consistently that I barely notice the added weight. When I take a beat and look around, I don't know where my personal insecurities end and ableism picks up. Who would I even be if my body were allowed seamless access to my city, my community, my friends' houses? I mean—really—what would happen if I stumbled onto some alternate universe made perfectly accessible to me? It's hard to imagine such an unfamiliar flow of confidence, self-assuredness, and ease.

* * *

The summer I moved back in with my parents drifted into fall, and finally, one of my desperate, late-night searches for a place to live brought up a little house with manageable rent and only a few front steps. I thought, *If I can find a way up that curb, and we build a ramp, maybe this could work?* I arranged a visit with the landlord. Micah bumped me up the front steps and through one of the two front doors. I took one look around, and my heart swooned. *Home!*

The landlord told me the house was built in 1895. All of the doorknobs were wobbly, and cracks were creeping up the walls and across the ceilings. It had a farmhouse kitchen sink, a free-standing claw-foot tub, and plenty of unexpected quirks (like that extra front door and ancient knobs on the vents and locks). I eyed the bathroom, and although I couldn't fit my chair through the door, the landlord said he'd throw up a few hand-rails. I could picture myself sitting on the edge of the tub while

I brushed my teeth at the sink. The real miracle was the washer and dryer located on the main level. In my previous house—as in most old houses—the laundry unit was located in the basement, so I'd been taking giant piles of dirty clothes over to my parents' house every other week for ages. A washer and dryer I could access in my own home! It was a palace. A few weeks later, I moved in and set to work making it my own.

Based on the design and (overwhelming lack of) flair breathed into the vast majority of tools and spaces deemed "accessible," I imagine it's assumed that disabled folks don't really have taste. If you need access, surely the desire for style has been canceled out. Accessibility must necessarily be the sole, all-consuming, number one priority, erasing any other possible preference or desire. "Beggars can't be choosers!" and all that. You'll take the glaring metal bars, cement walls, and brown Velcro, and you'll be grateful! Of course functionality is important. You might even say vital—I can't live somewhere that I can't get into. But I'm also a person with very specific preferences about floors and lighting, wall color and door frames in my home. I don't want just a shelter I can enter and survive in. I want a space that feels like home. Don't you?

Micah and I bought three flimsy, laminated bookshelves from the thrift store and spray-painted each piece on the front porch in the middle of the night. We gathered a bunch of old magazines, cut out piles of pictures, and pasted them onto pots and into collages for the walls. I placed my southwestern cactus lamp next to the giant Greek mythology painting with the gold frame, because I liked the way the colors meshed. Since I can't stand up for a shower very well, I reconfigured the space, hanging plants with hearty green leaves and winding vines along the shower curtain rod above the tub. Even today, I stare up at the vines curling above me during a soak and feel like I'm in a jungle. *Home!* The place where I feel inspired, free to create and dance and make messes and simply *be*—the place that swaddles me in stories and vibrant life.

Before I get carried away, and you start believing in happily-ever-after, it's important that we look at this house in its entirety. I love my cracking, wobbly home, but it's not a perfect picture of access. I park my car on the street, so I have to pop my wheelchair up on the curb, and I don't make it every time. Then I push myself up the steep ramp to my front door, which can be slow and grueling. Things fall off my lap, and it really sucks when it's raining. I can't fit my wheelchair in the bathroom, and my exquisite, freestanding tub is not an ideal setup for easy transfer. Falling is pretty routine.

Sometimes, after spilling my groceries trying to get up the ramp or slipping in the bathroom, I'll start another Craigslist search. *I've reached my limit!* I'll think. But quickly, the discouraging search to find a new accessible home I love and can afford brings back the warm fuzzies for where I am.

For now, I'm willing to pay the toll of the curb to feel cozy and inspired in my home. This is messy, works-for-now, finding-my-own-weird-way access, while not throwing aesthetics out the window. This is the balance I'm striking. For now. And for all of the intricacies, roadblocks, and trade-offs embedded in my own story, I see a library full of other stories—other ways folks with disabilities have managed to navigate the spaces they occupy. I don't know how many have landed in nursing homes. Who has died before their name made it to the top of one of those waiting lists? Who is going into debt, feeling ostracized, accumulating guilt for leaning on others? I don't know what badass accommodations people have built for themselves, what beautiful spaces have been dreamed into existence for disabled bodies and minds. I don't know all these stories, but I know each of them is full and complicated and deeply personal.

I understand that my city isn't actively trying to send me the message that I'm unwanted. The businesses in this area aren't forbidding me from spending my money there. My community isn't actively trying to make me move back in with my parents. That can't be said for a lot of groups of people throughout history and even today. Instead, the message I hear the most is something more like, "We're just not thinking about you at all"—a sentiment that intends no harm even as it dismisses an entire population.

✳ ✳ ✳

After waiting so long for the accessible dressing room, I feel empowered to use my voice. As I place my items on the checkout counter, I smile at the clerk and ask to speak with a manager. *I am not a threat! I just want to have a friendly chat,* my chirpy voice tells her in a frantic attempt to avoid slipping into the weatherworn role of Angry Cripple Versus Defensive Store Manager.

I don't know what I'm hoping for—that they'll put a lock on the door so you have to get a sales associate to let you in? That they post an extra threatening sign below the already existing "accessible" symbol?

"I just wanted to run something by you, so you and your staff can be aware," I say, smile fixed, treading so lightly. I explain that the accessible dressing room is often being used for extra-long fashion shows with pals. She is apologetic. Indignant, even. "That shouldn't happen," she says firmly. She seems to really feel it. I'm relieved. *She heard me,* I think.

"Next time you're in the store," she says, "let us know, and we'll make sure that room is available for you."

Wait, what? My hands tingle. The sturdy, clear communication I thought we were having completely dissolves. This is the solution? I imagine trying to flag down a staff member every time I visit the store. The awkwardness of getting their attention while a line of customers waits. Trying to explain the situation from the ground up to a new person each time. Shopping with the pressure of knowing they are keeping a dressing room open just for me.

It reminds me of the bakery in Westport with a lift outside the building that can be operated only with a key they keep inside. "Just call us when you're waiting outside. We'll send someone out to get you!" Or the crepe restaurant in Westside. After pushing yourself up the ramp attached to the side of the building, you find a locked door with a keypad. "Just send a friend to open it from the inside," they say. And what if I'm alone?

This moment in the thrift store waiting for the accessible dressing room is connected to a thousand other moments that—all together—weighs approximately one thousand pounds. But to the manager? This is a rare occasion. An unexpected hiccup in her week. Some disabled woman asking for a special favor each time she visits the store. It requires a small adjustment, an easy accommodation. Problem solved!

But to me and, I imagine, the aging woman who waited for the accessible room with me, this is an everyday, everywhere experience—the battle that follows the previous battle and precedes the next in our ongoing attempt to occupy space in the world.

"This isn't just about me," I tell the store manager. "This happens to everyone who comes in your store and needs that dressing room." She keeps nodding emphatically, sweetly even. The conversation fizzles into both of us repeating ourselves. She thinks she has heard me. I leave the store and get in my car, deflated. She didn't hear me at all.

✳ ✳ ✳

In that moment, talking with the thrift store manager, it felt clearer than ever—why stores are built the way they are, why nondisabled people perpetually occupy the few spaces designated for disabled bodies, why an entire city hadn't thought to build spaces for disabled folks to live in, why it's so hard to achieve genuine change: the vast majority of nondisabled people don't see—and certainly don't feel—the experience of disabled folks. There are others who recognize the textures of inaccessibility—fat and queer folks, so many aging bodies, people of color and those encountering language barriers, anyone who knows poverty—all have an extra set of fears, costs, and concerns.

But so many others can step into a new restaurant or bar
without worrying whether there will be a spot where they can
pee, and when they pop into that public restroom, they're presented with five stalls made with their bodies in mind. They can
click "accept" on an evite without researching venues and texting
the host to come up with an elaborate game plan for getting in
the door. They can get on and off public transportation, visit a
new city, travel from here to there without researching accessibility in advance. (Do you know how many destinations provide
any information about accessibility at all? Have fun on Google
with this one!) They can book a hotel room without worrying
whether they'll really be able to use the shower or sink once they
get there. They have access to every kind of seating in the theater,
stadium, coffee shop, bar. They can try on clothes in pretty much
every kind of dressing room ever made. When it's time to move,
they have more than literally one option. How can anyone feel
the rejection, reach, and urgency of inaccessibility if the entire
world has been built with them in mind?

Because inaccessibility over time equals . . . what, exactly? It's
more than a string of inconveniences. It's more powerful than a
missing ramp here and an elevator there. (Although, good lord,
I am grateful for every ramp and elevator I see. *Always*.) My
experience of inaccessibility is cumulative. It's more than a line
of targets to knock down. It's a way of being in the world, or just
outside of the world. It's a blaring message on a loudspeaker to
tune out. An ideology to survive.

Some days, I feel too vulnerable to leave my house, too fed

up to subject myself to the gamble of strangers interacting with me, too tired to fight to occupy a corner of space. Inaccessibility over time tells me that I do not matter, am not wanted, do not belong. This land wasn't made for me. So I stay in, keep to myself, avoid, cancel plans, carry anxiety in each fold and bend of my body, feel very alone and trapped and helpless. I also cope. I write, laugh, develop deep friendships with a safe few, find the movie theaters and coffee shops I can access and go to them one hundred times in a row, and sometimes I allow myself to be lifted up and down a flight of stairs. There are days I talk over the loudspeaker that says I'm not welcome, when I refuse to be invisible and silent. Sometimes, I even forget how hard this is. All of this is true at the same time.

Whenever I share a story about a shop that has a dumpster in its accessible parking spot or a restaurant that keeps its accessible entrance locked, people are quick to indignation, channeling all of their rage at this one business, listing all sorts of things I should do, or they would do, to demand accessibility. *You should call this number! I would tell off that person!* Some days, I have a bit of that fight in me. Especially when I can see the big picture—that this isn't just about me. Those days are the days I can talk to the manager about the problems I see with the thrift store's accessible dressing room. But the rest of the time?—it feels like getting out a toothbrush to clean a filthy house when I'm still trying to find a way to breathe in these rooms full of toxic fumes.

Even so. I choose to have faith that we are getting there, making our own weird way to an accessible future—a space that supports all of us. An accessible future is shaped by the fundamental understanding that we all have bodies, that those bodies are different from one another, and each is worthy of profound admiration, care, and respect. The aging body, the female body, the body in pain, the injured or sick body, the fat or short or asymmetrical body, the racially stigmatized body, the body that needs to use the bathroom, the blind, deaf, paralyzed, tired, nonbinary, hungry, bleeding, transitioning, seizing body. Every single one. In this future, people won't be punished, shamed, isolated, excluded, cast to the fringes, or told to go around the back or to find another toilet because of that body.

Bodies—in all of their variant forms—will be considered, allowed, and welcomed. Our vast differences will be thought of as we design our structures: our buildings, our healthcare, our transportation, our mobility aids, our roads, our governments, our clothing, our classrooms, our spaces of work and play, our notions of love and romance, parenthood and friendships. In this future, we will not be encouraged to silence our bodies. Instead of rejecting and abusing our bodies to fit into the boxes, our boxes will be bigger and malleable. This future doesn't only recognize but honors the fact that our bodies grow and tire and rebel and tremble and fight and change and scar and defy categorization. This future won't appear out of thin air; we have to create it—little by little—as we practice listening to, caring for, and respecting all of our bodies. Please. Let's create this world for each other.

EPILOGUE

As I worked on each chapter of this book, I kept wishing we were in the room together so I could hear your stories and questions, too—so we could think through all this together. And now that we're at the end, I especially wish we were face-to-face, because I have this pressing thing to say to you: *thank you.* For sitting with all these words, for receiving all of these stories, for making space to think through these ideas. Even if—especially if—parts of this book confused you or you found yourself sometimes talking back. You are some kind of miracle to me.

So, where do we go from here? How do we step into this unexplored accessible future together? How do we understand the power of representation and feel the weight of its absence? I believe we have to start with listening. We allow someone else's experiences—even when they differ from our own, *especially* when they differ from our own—to matter. We think critically about old, established narratives. We knock over some of the artificial boundaries we've invented for ourselves and see where the water flows. We try out new paths, and when those don't work, we find other ones.

If you're interested in doing this kind of reimagining, I've included below a messy pile of resources that have changed me in one way or another. I discovered some of this during my graduate work, some I read/watched with students, some I found through the cosmic powers of the Interwebs. This list is not exhaustive or focused, but it is entirely personal—I've included only creators/creations that I've spent time with and continue to think about today. My hope is that as we seek out these voices and draw them into our minds and communities, their insights will wash over us; change the way we look at, evaluate, and categorize each other; and prompt us to question our methods of determining human worth. I believe there is a kinder, more supportive, creative version of us out there, and listening to these voices is one way to move in that direction.

ACTIVISTS, ARTISTS, AND VERY COOL PEOPLE

IMANI BARBARIN

Creator of the powerful #WhenICallMyselfDisabled hashtag, Barbarin writes about the world we live in from the perspective of a Black woman with cerebral palsy. Whenever anything disability-related appears in the news or pop culture, I always want to know what Barbarin has to say about it. Follow her work at https://www.crutchesandspice.com.

EMILY LADAU

Disabled writer, speaker, and podcaster (check out *The Accessible Stall* podcast! It's worth your time), Ladau sees through all the bullshit and voices nuanced, honest insight into conversations being had about disability today. I mean, I referenced her work so many times while I defended my dissertation that it would have made for a great drinking game.

ALICE WONG

Wong is on the front lines of a movement as the director and founder of the @Disability_Visibility project (a collection of oral histories from people with disabilities), she started #Crip Lit (Twitter chats for disabled writers) and #CripTheVote (a nonpartisan movement to bring disabled voices into our politics), and she cocreated the Access Is Love project (an initiative to reframe and promote the expansion of access). She's a big deal, and you want to listen to what she has to say.

STELLA YOUNG

Revolutionary activist who coined the concept of "inspiration porn" in her TED Talk "I'm Not Your Inspiration, Thank You Very Much." Young is no longer with us, but her voice still carries so much power in the disability community.

BOOKS

ELI CLARE, *PRIDE AND EXILE: DISABILITY, QUEER-NESS, AND LIBERATION* (1999) AND *BRILLIANT IMPERFECTION: GRAPPLING WITH CURE* (2017)

Storyteller, activist, theorist, and poet who explores the intersections of disability, race, gender, sexuality, and class. I can't teach anything related to disability without bringing Clare into the conversation.

WILKIE COLLINS, *POOR MISS FINCH* (1872)

A hearty Victorian novel that tells a sensational story with a blind protagonist at the center. Collins very well might have been the first writer to place a disabled woman in the center of a story whose resolution is not found in a return to sight and who's portrayed as a desirable love interest, eventual mother, and powerful force. Hell, 150 years later, and he's *still* one of the only writers to tell this kind of story.

LUCY GREALY, *AUTOBIOGRAPHY OF A FACE* (1994)

American poet and memoirist who wrote the story of her life-long pursuit to correct her facial deformities through reconstructive surgeries. Thank you, Grealy, for giving us the gift of your unwavering insight before you left this world.

ALISON KAFER, *FEMINIST, QUEER, CRIP* (2013)

Theorist who writes stunning prose critically examining the relationship between disability and pop culture, current social and political events, and theoretical constructs. There is a before reading *FQC* and after reading *FQC*—I saw the world differently after reading this book.

ANDREW SOLOMON, *FAR FROM THE TREE: PARENTS, CHILDREN, AND THE SEARCH FOR IDENTITY* (2012)

Nonfiction writer and activist who follows his own openhanded curiosity to explore the intersections between marginalized identities. I am so grateful for the relentless nuance Solomon brings to the world; he takes nothing for granted, and I feel both brave and easy when I look at the world with his voice in mind.

TV SHOWS

SPECIAL

This Netflix miniseries tells the story of a gay man with cerebral palsy coming to terms with his own internalized ableism and facing the challenge of "coming out" as disabled to his coworkers. It's written and performed by the real-life protagonist of the story, Ryan O'Connell, and the story is full of moments that draw you into the pain and giggles of disabled living.

SPEECHLESS

This ABC comedy series tells the story of the zany, endearing DiMeo family, which includes JJ, a teenager with cerebral palsy. JJ's character is played by Micah Fowler, an actor with cerebral palsy. Creator Scott Silveri grew up with a brother who has CP, and his family was a lot like the family depicted in the show. The jokes are good and fresh and make me laugh, and the family sort of reminds me of my own weird family.

INSTAGRAM HASHTAGS

There are so many—I mean SO MANY—amazing disabled folks creating content on the internet, you guys. Once you start looking through these hashtags, I know you'll find and love them, too.

#DisabledAndCute
#DisabledAndBlack

#DisabledAndProud

#DisabledAndQueer

#DisabledAnd

#DisabledFashion

#DisabledJoy

#DisabledPeopleAreHot

#DisabledParent

#DisabledMom

#DisabledDad

#DisabilityVisibility

#DisabilityAwareness

#DisabilityInclusion

#AbleismExists

#AbleismIsTrash

#AccessIsLove

#BabeWithAMobilityAid

#CripplePunk

#HospitalGlam

#Spoonie

#SickGirlsClub

#SickChick

#TheFutureIsAccessible

#WhenICallMyselfDisabled

#NothingAboutUsWithoutUs

#365DaysWithDisability

POSTSCRIPT

The day after I submitted the final manuscript of this book—I mean, less than twenty-four hours after I hit "send" on this baby—Micah and I were bewildered to find out we were pregnant. (?!?!) As I shared with you only a few short pages before, we'd never known if my body could conceive. "You don't know until you know," my doctors always said.

Seven days later, Micah was diagnosed with colon cancer. This news was ten times *more*—shocking, petrifying, consuming.

The next few months turned into a blur of scans and peeing in cups. A surgeon, an oncologist, a radiologist, a dietitian, a high-risk OB, an SCI doctor, a pain specialist. Micah's tumor was declared stage 2 when I was eleven weeks pregnant. When the technician pulled out the jelly and wand at our first ultrasound, I was fully prepared for a somber voice to announce bad news. Instead, a tiny whale baby flashed across the screen—its speck of a heart winking back at us. "Everything is right on track!" the tech said. "Normal, normal, normal!" I'm not used to hearing this word attached to my body. "Really? Are you sure?" I was stunned, and annoyed by my own shock. Micah's tumor measured nearly 2 inches long; our fetus was 1.25 inches.

The story written for the handsome-faced, thirty-three-year-old man doesn't include colon cancer. The story written for the plucky disabled woman doesn't include caregiving and child-bearing. As Micah prepped for surgery and my body continued to expand with the growth of an entire human person, it never felt clearer: all of our bodies carry a multitude of strengths and frailties, and sometimes those are one and the same.

And then—you might remember this part—the entire globe reeled under the unprecedented spread of Covid-19. Micah was still recovering from surgery in the crowded ICU as we overheard the news coverage blaring from other patients' TVs. I sat in the rigid recliner next to Micah's bed, rubbing my belly—twenty-six weeks round—trying to understand what was happening, what any of it meant. A virus was spreading across the planet, and everyone passionately disagreed on what to do about it.

So much has changed—in my tiny world and the great wide world—since I wrote the first scattered words of this book. My partner's "healthy" body has revealed its own mortality. Even as he's recovering from surgery with a good prognosis, he's grappling with permanent changes in a body he'd always had the luxury of ignoring. My disabled body has flexed its majestic abilities. Even as my liver has faltered, my feet have swollen into shapes unrecognizable, and my bladder has required some extra maintenance and imagination, this pregnancy and our baby have followed a surprisingly typical trajectory. At the very same time, the virus has brought to the forefront the inherent frailties that come with living in a body (whether everyone has acknowledged it or not). Almost overnight, workplaces made themselves more flexible, more accessible. They created accommodations previously pitched as impossible. A giant portion of the American population suddenly found themselves uninsured, simply because a force entirely outside of their control decimated our economy. Hospital policy makers have grappled with whose lives to prioritize in their overcrowded floors, often revealing some of the ugliest ableist beliefs humans still hold close.

As I type these words, my restless baby kicks (and punches and rolls) against my forearms, reminding me he's coming to live in this world with us, and soon. I have multiple tabs open on my computer where I compulsively check the latest numbers of diagnoses and deaths. My swollen feet are propped up on a giant tub Micah scooted under my desk; like so many of our bodies these days, mine is strained and hanging on. And as I get ready for the birth of both my babies—human and book—I feel an added urgency behind the words I've gathered here. Things are changing, fast, and bringing the disabled body to the center of the conversation can only add much-needed, hard-earned insight, nuance, and practicality to the reimagining required of us. Insights like: sorting bodies into a hierarchy of those worth saving is an arbitrary and dangerous practice; health insurance should never be dependent on employment; collective collaboration will carry us so much further than individual pursuits. It's not that disabled people have all the answers to the problems unfolding around us—good lord, who does?—but if ever there was a time to invite us to the (figurative, social-distancing version of a) table, I'd say we've arrived.

ACKNOWLEDGMENTS

I am technically the author of this book, I know. My name is right there on the cover. But there are so many people who have helped labor *Sitting Pretty* into the world. It simply would not exist without the tender, sturdy care of an entire village.

Thank you to my partner, Micah, for reading every millimeter of every draft ever written for this book. I can see you, pacing from room to room with my laptop in your hands, reading paragraph after paragraph aloud, caring for these stories as if they were your own. I don't think I can imagine a greater expression of being seen and loved by another person.

Thank you to my parents for continuing to cheer for my writing (despite your gut aversion to every bit of "profanity" I spout across these pages). You've been through a whole lot with this youngest-born of yours, but your unwavering love and affirmation has been transformative.

Thank you to my siblings for being my first safe place—for giving me a picture of unfiltered acceptance I will never lose.

Thank you to the open and generous community I've found on Instagram. So much of my voice has been cultivated, post by post, with you. In the past few years, you created the space where I found the words to bridge the gap between the messy world around me and the tangle of feelings knotted inside me as you affirmed and bolstered, comforted and challenged me.

Thank you to my first writing mentor, Laura Moriarty, for seeing me as a writer before I could see it myself. If I had not collided with your creative energy when I did, I don't know if this book would ever have been written.

Thank you to my colleagues in the English department. Despite my relentless insecurities regarding the value of my writing—despite the absurdity of attempting to write a whole book while teaching teenagers every day—you never wavered in your enthusiasm, support, and celebration for this book.

Thank you to my friend and agent, Laura Lee Mattingly. I cannot believe you exist, let alone that we found each other. If I could have conjured my dream agent into existence, she would be you.

Thank you to my editor, Hilary Swanson. The first time we spoke, I felt the room fill with magic sparkles. You saw my vision for this book from its earliest blueprints and held it up for me when I lost my certainty. Thank you also to assistant editor Aidan Mahony, for writing the kinds of marginal comments that tricked me into forgetting that revising is a grueling process.

Thank you to all the disability scholars who interrogated the loudest status quo with sharp intellect and relentless imagination. Thank you for teaching me to do the same.

Thank you to all the disability activists who carried the weight, pushed against the barriers, and fought the battles that gave me the access I have today, not the least of which is my access to the very education that taught me to think and write and imagine this book into being.